POSITIVE TEACHING IN THE
PRIMARY SCHOOL

Dr Kevin Wheldall is Director of the Centre for Child Study at the University of Birmingham where Dr Frank Merrett is Honorary Research Fellow. They are the authors of *Positive Teaching: the behavioural approach* (1984), the BATPACK (1985) and BATSAC (1988) training packages and numerous research articles.

Effective Classroom Behaviour Management

POSITIVE TEACHING
IN THE
PRIMARY SCHOOL

FRA̶NK ̶M̶E̶R̶R̶E̶T̶T̶

KEV̶I̶N̶ ̶W̶H̶E̶L̶D̶A̶L̶L̶

First published 1990
Paul Chapman Publishing
144 Liverpool Road
London
N1 1LA

British Library Cataloguing in Publication Data

Merrett, Frank
  Positive teaching in the primary school. – (Effective
classroom behaviour management).
  1. Great Britain. Primary schools. Teaching
I. Title   II. Wheldall, Kevin, *1949–*   III. Series
372.11020941

  ISBN 1-85396-087-X

Printed and bound in Great Britain by
Athenaeum Press Ltd, Gateshead, Tyne & Wear.

D E F 6 5 4

CONTENTS

Preface   *vii*

Chapter 1. Identifying troublesome classroom behaviour   1

Chapter 2. Focusing on appropriate classroom behaviour   17

Chapter 3. Setting the classroom context   35

Chapter 4. Enhancing praise and reprimands   57

Chapter 5. Developing effective classroom strategies   76

Index   105

Preface

Problems of troublesome classroom behaviour start early. Some nursery and infant teachers claim that every year more and more young children starting school have behaviour problems and junior teachers frequently complain of lessons being disrupted by unacceptable behaviour.

The problem of disruptive behaviour in schools, generally, prompted the recent Enquiry into Discipline in Schools chaired by Lord Elton. This was initiated by the Secretary of State for Education in 1988 and we were invited to give evidence to the Committee as expert witnesses. In a sense, this book is a response to the recently published Elton Report, at least in the context of classroom behaviour problems in the primary school. The Elton Report refers to our research and recommends our package for training teachers in the skills of classroom behaviour management. We believe that problems of disruptive behaviour and indiscipline can be resolved, or at least reduced, by teachers learning to be both more sensitive and more positive in their interactions with children in school.

For over ten years we have been researching and disseminating what we refer to as Positive Teaching. This has included an extensive programme of research studies in nursery, infant and junior schools. We have examined the types of classroom behaviour primary teachers find particularly troublesome and have observed how they commonly react to such behaviour. More importantly, we have carried out experiments in primary schools to determine effective procedures for establishing good, positive classroom behaviour management.

Our programmes of research have greatly influenced our teaching. In order to provide effective training in Positive Teaching, we developed in-service training packages for teachers based on these findings. In 1985 we published our *Behavioural Approach to Teach-*

ing Package (BATPACK) for training primary teachers in classroom behaviour management. This was enthusiastically received. By releasing our package for wider use by other trained tutors we were able to satisfy the needs of more teachers.

In this book, we aim to provide an overview of our research and methods for those who have not been on one of our BATPACK courses and a useful summary for those who have. We should emphasise, however, that reading a book about Positive Teaching is no substitute for learning how to go about it. We learn new skills by practising them not by reading about them. The final chapter of this book contains a description of the BATPACK training package, on which this book, in part, is based. We would encourage readers to attend a BATPACK course in order to improve their skills in classroom behaviour management. By using Positive Teaching methods, primary school teachers can build less stressful and more effective teaching and learning environments. It is really quite straightforward, but for pupil behaviour to change, teachers must first change their own behaviour. This is the hard part but it can be done, as we show in this book.

We would like to thank our students for their enthusiastic support for Positive Teaching over the years. Many of the studies we report were carried out by students working under our supervision: mature, experienced teachers on in-service courses. We would also like to thank the following teachers for their helpful comments on draft chapters of this book: Steve Houghton, Jane Officer, Rod Parry and Jane Yeomans. We reserve to ourselves all responsibility for any blemishes or omissions that remain.

Frank Merrett and Kevin Wheldall, Winter, 1989

Chapter One
IDENTIFYING TROUBLESOME CLASSROOM BEHAVIOUR

If we were to believe some of the reports we read in the popular newspapers or see on television, we would be reluctant to venture into British primary schools. The picture is painted of insubordination and opposition, verbal abuse and even classroom violence. Teachers are presented as a beleaguered, oppressed group struggling against the barbarian hordes.

This view of contemporary schooling is frequently reinforced by the teachers' unions who, in their struggle for better pay and conditions, seem anxious to maintain this image of life in classrooms today. For example, the National Union of Teachers reported a survey in the summer of 1988, claiming that more than a third of teachers experience disrupted lessons as a result of indiscipline and that half of them believe that school discipline is a greater problem today than it was five years ago. Similarly, a *Daily Express* survey of members of the Professional Association of Teachers claims, on the basis of a survey carried out in 1987, that the vast majority (86%) of PAT members consider violence to be on the increase in schools and that 80% have experienced offensive verbal abuse. Primary teachers commenting on these findings confirmed that such problems were not restricted to the secondary sector:

> Violence among infant school pupils has certainly increased in my twenty years of teaching. Kicking and thumping are common. They re-enact Knightrider and the A-team (Crawley, infant teacher).

> Children arriving at school for the first time display aggressive tendencies and have obviously not been trained to listen. The disruptive element in classrooms is on the increase (Ayrshire, primary teacher).

> Children know that our hands are tied. We may not smack them, put them outside the door or, in some schools, keep them in at playtime or lunchtime. So there is nothing we can really do with the naughty child.....Parents cannot be bothered to discipline their children and look to us for an instant cure. With our hands tied this is difficult. However interesting the work set, some children persist in behaving badly. It is very depressing (Ruislip, junior teacher).

There is no doubt that some teachers are subjected to a great deal of stress. Over recent years teaching has undoubtedly become a more difficult business, requiring greater skill. But we should recognise that troublesome behaviour in children is not a new phenomenon. Take the following two examples.

> Children now love luxury. They have bad manners and contempt for authority. They show disrespect for their elders and love chatter in place of exercise; children are now tyrants, not the servants of their households.

> The world is passing through troubled times. The young people of today think of nothing but themselves. They have no reverence for their parents or for old age. They talk as if they alone know everything and what passes for wisdom with us is foolishness with them. As for the girls, they are foolish and immodest in speech, behaviour and dress.

In reading these words we could easily be listening to the views of some parents and teachers today or perhaps reading a *Daily Telegraph* editorial. But the first statement is attributed to Socrates and the second to Peter the Simple (1274). Clearly, it is important to keep a sense of proportion and to resist the flight into hysteria encouraged by the media.

In society at large a more liberal and generally less authoritarian attitude prevails today than even 20 or 30 years ago. This is reflected, if not actively welcomed, in many schools and many teachers are appreciative of the changed nature of the relationships they now enjoy with pupils. Some teachers are making more of an effort to relate to children in a less authoritarian way. But this has also led to serious challenges to authority for some teachers, perhaps especially those who have been less quick to adapt to the present, more relaxed, climate. Children today are less likely to live in fear of their teachers and will be more likely to react if treated harshly or unfairly.

These are important considerations for any approach to dealing with disruptive behaviour but before we can go much further we need to consider more carefully the nature of troublesome behaviour. Is the problem of schools really the high incidence of abusive and violent acts or is teacher stress caused by other forms of pupil behaviour? This was one of the questions addressed by the Elton Report on *Discipline in Schools* and our own recent research.

Which classroom behaviours do primary teachers say they find most troublesome?

Children with behaviour problems are a common type of referral to educational psychologists, and teachers frequently cite classroom behaviour problems as one of their major difficulties. However, there has been surprisingly little research concerned to identify the behaviours which classroom teachers find most troublesome. Various studies have attempted to determine prevalence rates of troublesome behaviour in children but the variation in reported incidence is considerable, varying from about 5% to over 25%. It is clear either that behaviour problems fluctuate unpredictably in incidence or, more likely, the definition of behaviour problems varies considerably across studies. Our own concern has been with identifying what teachers regard as troublesome behaviour in the classroom. We were interested to know not only what proportion of primary aged children are behaviourally troublesome to teachers but also just what these troublesome behaviours are.

Before describing our research there are several important aspects of the problem of classroom behaviour that we need to consider. First, there is the question of emphasis. Previous research has tended to be concerned almost exclusively with identifying the incidence of children with behaviour problems. Consequently, the children have been the focus, rather than the behaviour. Our emphasis is upon the behaviour itself. Second, there is the need to define and describe the relevant behaviours which make up the rag-bag category of troublesome behaviour. If we use vague, catch-all phrases we must not be surprised if we find variations in incidence. Moreover, what is disturbing to one teacher may be quite acceptable to another, which emphasises the importance of objective definition of an array of specific behaviours which teachers may find troublesome. Third, there is the question of the severity of the problem behaviour as against the rate at which it occurs. There is no doubt that an incident of stabbing in the classroom is to be regarded as extremely severe but, thankfully, such events are rare. On the other hand, a relatively trivial offence such as calling out may occur so frequently that the lesson dissolves into total chaos. So it is necessary to consider both the degree of troublesomeness and the frequency of problem behaviours.

We attempted to determine what teachers themselves believed to be the most frequent and the most troublesome disruptive behaviours occurring in primary school classrooms. Teachers completed (anonymously) a questionnaire which sought information on their age, sex and length of teaching experience. The questionnaire then posed a series of questions related to classroom behaviour problems. The first asked, "Do you feel that you spend more time dealing with problems of order and control than you ought?" The next three questions were concerned with identifying which of the ten categories of disruptive behaviour listed in the table on page 5 were a) most frequent and b) most troublesome. This was first asked in general terms and then with reference to individual children selected by each teacher as being particularly troublesome.

The questionnaire was distributed to 32 primary schools chosen at random from one West Midlands local education authority to give a 25% sample. Sufficient survey forms were sent to every school in the sample so that each full-time class teacher could complete the questionnaire. Replies were received from all 32 schools involved, resulting in a very high return rate (93% overall). Of the 198 teachers replying 73% were women and all age ranges were represented fairly evenly.

Half of our sample (51%) responded affirmatively to the question "Do you think that you spend more time on problems of order and control than you ought?" The same percentages of women and men responded in this way and there were no major differences between the responses of older and younger teachers or between teachers of younger and older pupils.

The categories of misbehaviour employed in the primary survey

A	Eating	Chewing gum, paper or equipment, eating sweets in class.
B	Making unnecessary noise (non-verbal)	Banging objects/doors, scraping chairs, moving clumsily.
C	Disobedience	Refusing/failing to carry out instructions or to keep class or school rules.
D	Talking out of turn	Calling out, making remarks, interrupting and distracting others by talking or chattering.
E	Idleness/slowness	Slow to begin or finish work, small amount of work completed.
F	Unpunctuality	Late to school/lessons, late in from playtime/break.
G	Hindering other children	Distracting others from their work, interfering with their equipment or materials.
H	Physical aggression	Poking, pushing, striking others, throwing things.
I	Untidiness	In appearance, in written work, in classroom, in desks.
J	Out of seat	Getting out of seat without permission, wandering around.

The average class size taught was 27. On average, 4.3 pupils were regarded as troublesome by their class teachers and of these 3.0 were boys. When teachers were asked to pick out the two most troublesome individual children in the classes, boys were identified as the most troublesome by 76% and as the next most troublesome by 77%. This supports the anecdotal view that boys, generally, tend to be regarded as more troublesome than girls.

What was it that these children did that was troublesome? As we said earlier, it was the type and frequency of troublesome behaviours in which we were particularly interested. When asked to pick out the most *troublesome* behaviour 46% of primary teachers cited talking out of turn (TOOT) and 25% cited hindering other children (HOC). None of the other categories reached over 10%, as the bar graph on page 7 shows.

The findings for the most *frequent* troublesome behaviours gave a broadly similar picture and when we went on to ask about the troublesome behaviours of individual children, again we got the same response, TOOT followed by HOC. These two categories are not particularly serious misbehaviours but they give rise to a great deal of nagging and to other negative teacher responses. The category physical aggression was cited by only 5% of teachers as being the most troublesome behaviour and by only one per cent as being the most frequent. Physical violence appears to be a problem encountered by relatively few teachers but many, if not most, have their job made more stressful by the petty misbehaviours which we have identified. Even for the most troublesome children the key behaviours identified were not particularly serious or problematic.

In passing we should note that a parallel survey we conducted with secondary school teachers reached very similar conclusions, TOOT and HOC again being selected as the most troublesome behaviours. Contrary to popular belief, secondary school pupils are not necessarily more badly behaved but, in fact, continue to display many of the same troublesome behaviours as at primary school.

Percentages

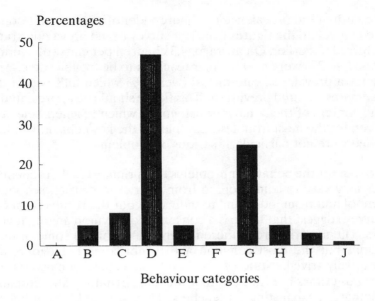

Behaviour categories

Most troublesome behaviours

What may we conclude from these results? We would appear to be safe in assuming that the classroom behaviour problems experienced by most primary school teachers are not of a serious nature. TOOT and HOC appear to be the two misbehaviours which teachers generally identify as causing them the most trouble and as occurring most often. These findings are broadly confirmed by the larger-scale replication study, involving 3,500 teachers, commissioned for the Elton Report which was inspired by our research. This is not to say that serious incidents do not occur occasionally in some schools but they are certainly not as frequent as the media would have us believe. Physical violence appears to be a problem encountered (thankfully) by relatively few teachers but many, if not most, teachers have their job made more stressful by the petty misbehaviours we have identified.

Regarding the prevalence of children identified as troublesome, we may relate the figures from our survey to the prevalence rates referred to earlier. On average, 4.3 children per class (of average class size 27) were said by their teachers to be troublesome. This yields a prevalence rate of just over 15% which falls within the estimates we cited previously. This figure should be appreciated in the context of the behaviour categories which teachers selected. Even for the most troublesome children the key behaviours identified were not particularly serious or problematic.

To sum up, the behaviour problems that primary teachers encounter may vary to some degree from district to district, school to school and from individual to individual but the results from our survey suggest that there is a consensus of opinion among teachers. The majority are bothered by the behaviour of some of their pupils but the most common and troublesome behaviours are relatively trivial. None of the key troublesome behaviours are serious crimes but they are time-wasting, irritating, stressful and, ultimately, exhausting for teachers. They are the kinds of behaviours which elicit the litany of reprimands and desist commands heard so frequently in classrooms. The good news is that these are the very behaviours which respond well to simple, positive methods of classroom behaviour management as we will show in this book.

Causes of troublesome behaviour

In our view there has been an excessive pre-occupation with the so-called causes of misbehaviour. Teachers and parents are often very quick to give reasons why they think children misbehave in class even if, as is usually the case, they are only guessing. The reasons teachers commonly give for difficult behaviour can be thought of in a number of ways depending on whether they see the reason as being somehow within the children themselves, stemming from their home backgrounds or the kind of neighbourhood in which they are living or, perhaps, from their school or classroom situations. In the table on page 9 we give examples of the sort of reasons sometimes given for talking out of turn (TOOT) and hindering other children (HOC), according to these categories.

Behaviour problem	Causes within the pupil	Causes within the family or neighbourhood	Causes within the school or class setting
TOOT	extroverted a bit thick neurotic	large family poor diet TV always on	work too easy directions unclear seating
HOC	aggressive brain-damaged insecure	violent father council housing spoilt at home	lack of space poor teaching no clear rules

In our view, many of the causes or reasons given in the first two columns do not bear close scrutiny. To say that Darren interferes with the work of others because he is aggressive does not get us very far. It is a label which merely substitutes different words to describe the behaviour. We call such labels given for troublesome behaviours *explanatory fictions*. Take the following conversation between two teachers, for example,

"Jenny Stevens has always got a lot to say for herself. Rabbit, rabbit, rabbit - she never stops talking! I wish I knew why."

"Well, you see, the reason is that Jenny is a classic extrovert, that's why."

"How do you know that?"

"It's obvious. Extroverts are very sociable types who like to talk a lot."

This is just a circular argument and gets nowhere. Giving a fancy label to a misbehaviour does not help us to solve the problem. Some educational psychologists have been irritating teachers by doing this sort of thing for years!

Some reasons given may be all too real but there is little that we as teachers can do about such causes. Jenny may watch too many video nasties, eat too much junk food, come from a family of seven, have an unresolved Electra complex and/or be suffering from minimal brain damage but there is little that we can do directly to resolve any of these difficulties even if they are influencing her classroom behaviour. We cannot ask Jenny to hop on the couch and tell us about her dreams nor would advice to her parents on birth control or healthy eating be very effective. We are teachers not social workers or psychiatrists. We do best to concentrate on reasons where we have very much more influence.

To take this position is not to deny the importance of, nor to deny the interest of the teacher in, the home or in co-operation with parents but we must accept our limitations. Similarly, we accept that pupils' personal problems will sometimes affect their behaviour in school. We, as teachers, know from personal experience how our day's work in schools can be affected by, say, an argument at breakfast time. Clearly, sympathy for and an understanding of the personal and social difficulties of children are essential characteristics of caring, positive teachers but these may not be enough. Whilst we cannot necessarily do much to alleviate personal problems or counter the effects of poor social conditions, we can strive to create positive, responsive environments for pupils in our classrooms where we have more control over many of the elements. Such environments provide warmth and acceptance within a climate of clear rules and expectations and opportunities for engaging in activities which provide positive feedback.

If we look back at the third column in our table we can see that many of these possible causes of misbehaviour are amenable to resolution by action on the part of the teachers. We can make sure that the work we set is at an appropriate level. We can negotiate with our pupils some effective, positive rules for appropriate conduct in the classroom. We can ensure that the seating arrangements are suitable for the work we have set and that we use the space available to the best advantage. We can learn to be more observant of pupil behaviour, both good and bad, and to respond to it appropriately. Positive teachers realise that they have a great deal of influence over key factors in the classroom. This is not always used as effectively as it might be by many teachers and in this book we will discuss how Positive Teaching methods may be employed to resolve classroom behaviour difficulties.

The five principles of Positive Teaching

Positive Teaching is based on five basic principles. The aim is to promote good classroom practice by, almost exclusively, positive methods. Our concern in this book is with effective classroom behaviour management but this is not meant to imply that Positive Teaching does not have an equally important role to play in teaching academic skills such as reading and writing. We will be concerned here, however, exclusively with the use of Positive Teaching methods to manage pupils' social behaviour. We should note, however, that it is generally accepted that appropriate behaviour in the classroom is necessary for academic learning to take place. Children have little opportunity to learn if they are continually being disrupted or if they themselves are continually disrupting the teacher or other pupils.

1. Teaching is concerned with the observable.

Positive teachers concern themselves with what children actually do rather than speculating about unconscious motives or processes which may be thought to underlie their pupils' behaviour. The only evidence we have about what people can do or will do and about what they believe comes to us by observing their behaviour. Consequently, careful definition and observation of behaviour are central to the behavioural approach. As we have already noted, teachers frequently propose explanations for behaviour which are not reasons at all but merely labels or explanatory fictions. To say that Barry or Imran is often out of his seat because he is hyperactive is, quite simply, circular and gets us nowhere; the expression hyperactive is just another word to describe the same behaviour. It does nothing to explain it and provides no help in solving the problem. Indeed, such labels are often used as an excuse for doing nothing.

2. Almost all classroom behaviour is learned.

Positive teachers do not deny genetic inheritance nor do they assume that anybody can be taught to do anything given time. Genetic inheritance may set the limits for what an individual can learn, but behaviour is still largely the result of learning. Certainly this applies to the sort of behaviour that teachers are chiefly concerned with, such as knowing how to respond politely to others or being able to read. Of course, pupils learn bad behaviour as well as good behaviour. The good news is that bad behaviour can be unlearned and new, more appropriate behaviour learned in its place.

3. Learning involves change in behaviour.

The only way that we know (that we can know) that learning has taken place is by observing change in a pupil's behaviour. Positive teachers will not be satisfied with vague statements such as, "Gemma has a better attitude towards school now". Evidence is needed that she now attends on time, answers more questions, completes her work more quickly or whatever. These are all clear examples of behaviours which can, if necessary, be counted and compared.

4. Behaviour changes as a result of its consequences.

This means that we all (pupils and teachers) learn on the basis of tending to repeat behaviours which are followed by consequences we find desirable or rewarding. We tend not to repeat behaviours, the consequences of which we find aversive or punishing. If we wish to change the behaviour of our pupils we should concentrate upon arranging for desirable consequences to follow appropriate behaviour. It has been shown repeatedly that rewarding appropriate behaviour is a more effective way of bringing about change than punishing undesirable behaviour.

5. Behaviours are also influenced by classroom contexts.

In any situation some behaviours are more appropriate than others. If a pupil's behaviour is appropriate for a particular circumstance then it is likely to be rewarded by the people (adults or peers) who are around. If it is inappropriate to the situation it is less likely to be rewarded and may even be punished. As a result pupils rapidly learn not only how to behave in certain ways but also when and where such behaviours are appropriate. Certain behaviours are more likely in some situations rather than others simply because there is more opportunity to engage in them. For example, there is far more chance to chatter and to interfere with others when seated in classroom table groups than when in rows. It is necessary to consider classroom antecedents for behaviour as well as consequences. We will consider these aspects in more detail later.

These five principles sum up what we mean by Positive Teaching. The main assumption is that pupils' behaviour is primarily learned and maintained as a result of their interactions with their environment, which includes other pupils and teachers. Consequently, behaviour can be changed by altering certain features of that environment. As we have said, the key environmental features are events which immediately precede or follow behaviour. This means that classroom behaviours followed by consequences which the pupils find rewarding will tend to increase in frequency. Similarly, certain changes in behaviour may be brought about merely by changing the classroom setting.

If we believe that teaching is concerned with helping pupils to learn new skills and gain new information, and if we believe also that learning implies some sort of change in behaviour, then it follows logically that teaching is about changing behaviour. If teaching is about changing behaviour then the role of the teacher is, quite simply, to bring about changes in the behaviour of the pupils in his or her class.

Justifying our actions

But what right have we to play God? How can we justify our actions when seeking to change pupils' behaviour? Questions such as these cannot be shirked; if we do not ask them of ourselves, then sooner or later someone else will.

The first point we can make is that Positive Teaching is honest and straightforward in so far as it encourages teachers to examine a troublesome problem, to define it clearly, to state their aims and the means by which they are attempting to bring about change. Before teachers can decide whether they need to take action over a certain behaviour they must decide upon the appropriateness of it in the classroom context. Teachers must be able to justify their actions in terms of the long-term benefits for their pupils. Some pupil behaviour may be annoying to the teacher but not, in itself, harmful. For example, chewing in class, though it may be judged to be disrespectful by some teachers, could not be said to be wrong, unless dietary or other considerations are taken into account. If we can agree that the teacher's main task is to arrange for learning to take place, then within the context of the classroom any behaviour can be judged inappropriate if it:

1. interferes with the child's own learning,

2. interferes with the learning of other members of the class or,

3. prevents the teacher from getting on with his or her job of instructing, explaining, reading, organising, coaching and so on.

Thus day-dreaming, playing with materials or apparatus or wandering around the room would certainly interfere with the pupil's own learning. Talking to others in the group or attacking them or their property would clearly interfere with the learning of others, whilst persistent conduct of this nature would probably demand a great deal of the teacher's time and attention, preventing much effective teaching from going on. Much of the teacher's concern is to see that the children concentrate or get on with the job in hand; what is known as *on-task* behaviour. If the pupils are not on-task then the likelihood is that not much learning is going on. In fact, recent research has shown a clear relationship between on-task behaviour and the amount of classwork completed. If we can increase on-task behaviour then at least learning is possible, providing always that the material is appropriate to the pupil's current skill level. The main aim of this book is with the management of children's classroom behaviour, which inevitably yields improved academic behaviour.

Some critics might argue that Positive Teaching merely attempts to treat the symptoms (the behaviour) rather than the underlying problem itself. Such approaches, they claim, are akin to prescribing aspirin for toothache, which alleviates the symptoms (pain) but leaves the real cause (a rotten tooth) untreated. As a result of this, they would argue, other symptoms (problems) will inevitably surface sooner or later. In classroom terms this would be illustrated by a child who, when taught to remain seated instead of wandering about the classroom, will now begin calling out to the teacher or displaying other unwanted behaviours, since the cause is left untreated. This is sometimes referred to as symptom substitution. In response to this, we would argue that:

1. the behaviour is the problem

2. supposedly deeper causes are frequently difficult to identify and often take the form of explanatory fictions, and

3. there is no experimental evidence to suggest that if we remove one problem another one will appear to replace it.

In sum, Positive Teaching concerns itself with the observable. There are no inner mysteries, the approach is direct and the outcomes clear. In the final analysis we point to our success rate in achieving enduring changes in behaviour without any evidence for symptom substitution or any other side-effects.

Finally, there is the issue of so-called bribery. Because rewards and praise are important parts of the Positive Teaching repertoire, the charge of bribery is sometimes levelled at our approach. This glib charge is easily challenged since bribery usually means to give someone an inducement in advance to do something immoral or illegal! In Positive Teaching praise and rewards are, essentially, given following appropriate behaviour which the teacher has determined is in the pupil's long-term interests. To call such behaviour bribery makes as much sense as saying that teachers have to be bribed for working with a monthly pay cheque!

Further reading

Our survey of troublesome classroom behaviour in primary schools is reported fully in:

Wheldall, K. and Merrett, F. (1988). Which classroom behaviour problems do primary school teachers say they find most troublesome? *Educational Review, 40,* 13-27.

For a broad perspective on the question of disruptive behaviour in schools teachers should consult the Elton Report:

Department of Education and Science (1989). *Discipline in Schools.* London: H.M.S.O.

Chapter Two
FOCUSING ON APPROPRIATE CLASSROOM BEHAVIOUR

Problems of classroom behaviour and poor motivation are endemic in education. Teachers consistently cite difficulties in these two areas as their main classroom concerns and traditionally they have been dealt with in the same way, that is, by punitive methods. Both unacceptable or troublesome behaviour and idleness or lack of interest represent threats to the teacher's role which he or she commonly seeks to prevent by aversive means. One consequence of this may be the daily repetition of desist commands heard in many classrooms: "Sit down, Nadia. Talking again, Narinder. Leave Brendon alone, Nigel - get on with your own work. Something of interest outside, Mary? Eyes on your work please," and so on, endlessly. Teachers become very good at noticing and commenting on the disruptive behaviour of their pupils (in a sense they feel forced to do so) and for a number of reasons they feel that they have to respond.

Teachers the world over spend a considerable proportion of their teaching time reprimanding pupils for troublesome and/or non-work-related behaviours as we shall see. They hardly ever comment approvingly on appropriate behaviour. As we have already shown, teachers are mostly concerned with high frequency but relatively trivial troublesome behaviours such as talking out of turn and hindering other pupils. These are the behaviours which help to cause teacher stress as they occur with monotonous regularity and result in immediate reaction which usually takes the form of reprimands and sanctions. We believe that teachers should *act* rather than *react* in the classroom. To react on the spur of the moment may be natural; but is it professional and is it effective? This surely is the difference between a professional and a lay response to children's behaviour.

The phasing out of corporal punishment in our schools has been accompanied by renewed interest in seeking out alternative methods of achieving good classroom discipline. In our research on Positive Teaching we have concentrated on how teachers should behave in classrooms in order to bring about suitable conditions for effective and efficient learning to take place. We have been concerned with problems of troublesome classroom behaviour and with methods of encouraging pupils to behave in ways which will maximise their opportunities for learning appropriate academic skills and knowledge. We have shown teachers how to encourage and increase the kinds of behaviour they want to see their pupils engaged in and which are of educational benefit to them. In order to do this, teachers need to know more about behaviour, its antecedents and its consequences.

The ABC of Positive Teaching

The crucial elements of Positive Teaching are as simple as ABC.

A refers to the antecedent conditions, i.e. the context in which a behaviour occurs or what is happening in that environment prior to a behaviour occurring.

B refers to the behaviour itself, i.e. what a pupil is actually doing in real physical terms (not what you think he or she is doing as a result of inferences from his or her behaviour).

C refers to the consequences of the behaviour, i.e. what happens to the pupil after the behaviour.

Let us look at these three elements again in a little more detail, beginning with behaviour. We will return to the topic of antecedents in Chapter Three.

Behaviour. We have already said that pupils' behaviour refers to what they are actually doing and positive teachers attempt to say what they are doing in as precise a way as possible. If we observe a pupil looking at a book, we would not write down studying since another observer or someone else reading our notes might interpret studying differently. It is too vague and imprecise. We might record that the pupil was looking at the book and turned over five pages in a period of three minutes but to say that this is studying is to interpret. Such interpretation is prone to inaccuracy and vagueness and is unlikely to be useful. Similarly, if a teacher tells us that Jason is always "messing about" in class, we have to ask the teacher to define that behaviour more clearly. What we regard as messing about may not be what the teacher regards as messing about. Moreover, if we use a vague definition there is no guarantee that it is the same sort of behaviour we are categorising in this way two days running. So we would ask the teacher to list any of Jason's behaviours which he or she finds objectionable and then to define them as precisely as possible. This is known as *pin-pointing.*

As we have seen, talking out of turn is frequently found at the top of many teachers' lists of troublesome behaviours. If we define this as "any non-work-related talking by pupils when the teacher has requested the class to get on with set work quietly", then we are moving closer towards an objective definition. The more objective our definition, the easier it is for two observers to agree that a certain behaviour has occurred and the easier it is to count instances of such behaviour. Counting instances of behaviour is an extremely important component of Positive Teaching because comparison of such counts allows us to see what is happening when we try to bring about change over a period of time. Precise definition of behaviour also helps us to avoid the danger of over-interpretation and giving explanatory fictions as causes of behaviour. These are generally unhelpful and give a veneer or gloss of scientific explanation.

Consequences. As we said earlier, this refers to the fact that we (and that means all of us, pupils and teachers alike) tend to repeat behaviours which bring us what we want and to refrain from repeating behaviours leading to events which we want to avoid. Almost everyone learns to find praise and approval rewarding and will tend to behave in a way which is likely to be followed by praise or approval. A major concern within Positive Teaching is with the identification of items and events which pupils find rewarding and to structure the teaching environment so as to make access to these rewards dependent upon behaviour which the teacher wants to encourage in class. This is what we mean by acting rather than reacting.

In simple everyday language consequences may be described as rewarding or punishing. Rewarding consequences, which we call *positive reinforcers*, are events which we seek out or "go for", whilst we try to avoid *punishing* consequences. Neutral consequences are events which affect us neither way. Behaviours followed by positive reinforcers are likely to increase in frequency. Behaviours followed by punishers tend to decrease in frequency whilst neutral consequences have no effect. In Positive Teaching, infrequent but appropriate behaviours (for example, getting on with the set work quietly) are made more frequent by arranging for positive reinforcers, such as teacher attention and approval, to follow their occurrence. In the environment of the classroom the teacher is responsible for providing many of the consequences for the behaviour of pupils. Teachers do this in a number of ways but chiefly by responding to their pupils' behaviour and their work in terms of feedback, through words and actions. This is called *social reinforcement.*

Undesired behaviours may be decreased in frequency by ensuring that positive reinforcers do not follow their occurrence, i.e. a neutral consequence is arranged. Occasionally it may be necessary to follow undesired behaviours with punishers (for example, a quiet reprimand) in an attempt to reduce the frequency of behaviour rapidly but there are problems associated with this procedure. Punishment plays only a minor and infrequent role in Positive Teaching not least because sometimes what we believe to be punishing is, in fact, reinforcing to the pupil. Pupils who receive little attention from adults may behave in ways which result in adult disapproval. Such pupils may prefer disapproval to being ignored and will continue to behave like this because adult attention, in itself, whether praise or reprimand, is positively reinforcing. This is what some people call attention-seeking behaviour.

We should note that terminating a punishing consequence is also reinforcing and can be, and often is, used to increase desired behaviours. This is known as *negative reinforcement*. Again this has problems associated with its use since pupils may rapidly learn other, more effective, ways of avoiding the negative consequence than you had in mind. For example, some teachers continually use sarcasm and ridicule with their pupils. They cease only when their pupils behave as they wish. Another way for pupils to avoid this unpleasant consequence, however, other than by doing as the teacher wishes, is to skip lessons or stay away from school.

Finally, one can punish by removing or terminating positive consequences (for example, by taking away privileges). This is known as *response cost* but again there are similar problems associated with this. Pupils may find alternative ways of avoiding this unpleasant consequence. Lying, cheating and shifting the blame are common strategies employed. These are all behaviours we would wish to discourage but by creating consequences which we believe to be aversive we may be making them more likely to occur.

When we want to teach pupils to do something new, or to encourage them to behave in a certain way more frequently than they normally do, it is important that we ensure that they are positively reinforced every time they behave as we want them to. This normally leads to rapid learning and is known as continuous reinforcement. When they have learned the new behaviour and/or are behaving as we want them to do regularly, then we may maintain this behaviour more economically by reducing the frequency of reinforcement.

Another important reason for wanting to reduce the frequency of reinforcement is that pupils may become less responsive if the positive reinforcer becomes too easily available. Consequently, once pupils are regularly behaving in an appropriate way we can best maintain that behaviour by ensuring that they are now reinforced only intermittently. Intermittent reinforcement can be arranged so that pupils are reinforced every so often (i.e. in terms of time) or, alternatively, after so many occurrences of the behaviour. These different ways of organising the frequency of reinforcement are known as reinforcement schedules and we need to bear these considerations in mind when we are applying the principles of Positive Teaching in the classroom. We shall consider these points again in Chapter Five.

With some pupils the behaviour that concerns us has not yet been learned, so our job is to teach it. With others, the behaviour is learned but does not occur frequently enough. Other pupils frequently behave in inappropriate ways. Positive Teaching is about changing the frequency of behaviour. It can be used to teach new skills or to increase or decrease existing rates of behaviour. It is important to emphasise that Positive Teaching is primarily concerned with increasing the frequency of appropriate behaviour in the classroom rather than with reducing disruptive behaviour *per se*. In a sense, this leads to the same outcome. Since a person can engage in only one sort of activity at a time, if we increase the time spent profitably, we must reduce the opportunities for misbehaviour.

It should also be emphasised that Positive Teaching is not about creating robots who just do as they are told, mindlessly following the teacher's instructions. Rather, Positive Teaching is about helping children to become effective independent learners. We certainly do not advocate approaches requiring rigid adherence to curricula based on behavioural objectives, for example, as we have argued elsewhere, in the book *Effective Classroom Learning*. Positive teachers should, in effect, like all good teachers, have the ultimate aim of making themselves redundant.

How do primary teachers typically behave in the classroom?

Teachers are in general agreement with the view that, where possible, their interactions with children should be positive, involving the use of praise, rather than negative, involving the use of reprimands. This is altogether more agreeable for both teachers and pupils. Nobody thrives in a situation where one party is always chiding the other and where conflict remains barely concealed beneath the surface.

In a recent survey of opinion we carried out among teachers we found that all of them agreed that it is better to be encouraging towards pupils rather than to nag and chide them. A common reaction to our suggestion to teachers that they should improve their use of praise and encouragement is, "Ah, but we do that already". Of the teachers in the survey mentioned above, 90% thought that they were more positive than negative in dealing with their pupils. We wanted to know whether this was, in fact, true and how far this common attitude was carried through in teachers' behaviour. In other words, do they use more praise than blame?

We arranged for a large sample of British primary school teachers to be observed interacting with their classes in schools in the West Midlands. Our trained observers, using specially prepared observation schedules, watched 128 teachers and their 5 to 11 year-old pupils. Teachers and their classes were observed at different times during the day and week on at least three separate occasions for half an hour.

Our observation schedule entitled OPTIC (Observing Pupils and Teachers In Classrooms) samples teachers' use of praise and disapproval and the behaviour of their classes. Observers record the number of times teachers give praise or reprimands to pupils and whether these are in response to pupils' academic work or their social behaviour. The schedule also allows an estimate to be made of the amount of time pupils spend behaving appropriately; for example, actually getting on with the work set by the teacher (or time on-task, as we call it).

The good news is that, on average, this sample of primary pupils spent about 70% of their time on-task and this is in line with the estimates of other observers. (This compares with 80% on-task in a similar sample of secondary classes we observed.) In two thirds of the primary classes children spent between 57% and 83% of their time engaged in activities defined as appropriate by their teachers.

Overall, teachers were much more positive than negative in their responses to pupils' academic work (see the table on page 24). On average teachers used three times as much praise as disapproval.

When commenting on pupils' classroom behaviour, however, teachers used nearly five times as much disapproval as approval. Approval for social behaviour was very rare; 38 (nearly 30%) of the teachers observed gave none at all. Pupils are clearly expected to behave well and are continually reprimanded if they do not. In our view, much of this negative responding to classroom behaviour by teachers is ineffective and may, in fact, be counter-productive.

Approval to and disapproval of academic work and classroom behaviour expressed as percentages of all teacher responses

	Approval to	Disapproval of	Totals
Academic work	50	16	66
Classroom behaviour	6	28	34
Totals	56	44	100

Children in the older junior classes were taught by roughly equal numbers of men and women teachers. Consequently, we were able to compare the results for male and female teachers but we found the differences to be very small and none was significant. Men and women teachers in primary classes would seem to behave in very much the same way.

It appears then that the most common way primary school teachers have of dealing with disruptive and inappropriate behaviour is to reprimand offending pupils rather than to encourage more appropriate classroom behaviour. A similar pattern is reflected in the systems many primary schools employ to regulate pupils' behaviour. For example, nearly all schools have a number of rules, sometimes called guidelines, which all too frequently consist of a list of "Thou shalt nots". They rarely specify acceptable and appropriate pupil behaviour. Such rules are generally upheld by sanction systems of increasing severity whilst reward systems are seldom employed to maintain appropriate behaviour. Good behaviour is expected and, therefore, ignored when it does occur. Schools do employ reward systems of some sort but they rarely focus on appropriate behaviour after the early years. There is no doubt at all that teachers and the school environment generally, provide many consequences for the behaviour of pupils which are negative and, in a sense, punishing.

Why are teachers so negative?

Why then do primary teachers and schools operate in such a negative fashion? One reason is that reprimands appear to work, and to work instantly. If a teacher shouts at a pupil to sit down or to stand up straight he or she will often respond at once. After a short while, however, the pupil may well be standing up or slouching once again but the immediate effect of the rebuke is rewarding for the teacher who will tend to repeat that sort of behaviour since it appeared to work. Secondly, we as teachers and parents are very good at spotting pupils behaving in ways that we object to, and feel that we have to respond at once. It has become a habit with us. Pupils, too, come to expect teachers to behave in this way towards them and if they do not do so they tend to brand such teachers as being soft. Generally, this is the way society is organised in that good behaviour is expected of us and goes unremarked whilst if we are caught doing something against the law we are punished. In the same way, teachers expect their pupils to behave well and tend to ignore them when behaving appropriately. It was, after all, the way that most teachers were treated when they were pupils themselves. On occasion, teachers may get frustrated and stressed and act without thinking. In any case, it is difficult to catch children behaving well especially if they do not do it very often. Many teachers are not convinced that it is necessary to attend to appropriate behaviour. Furthermore, to do it well requires practice.

Disadvantages and side-effects of reprimands and punishment

These then may be some of the reasons why teachers tend to be negative towards their pupils. However, there are numerous disadvantages and practical problems which arise if the systems and methods employed by schools and teachers are essentially punitive and many unwanted side-effects are associated with them. First, prohibitive rules serve only to define what will not be tolerated but give no indication of alternative, appropriate behaviours. As mentioned above a rebuke or punishment may appear to work in the short term thus encouraging the adult to persevere with such a response. But for some children the attention they get when they offend is the only attention they ever get. When they do conform they are ignored and if attention is what they need (and which of us does not?) then pupil and teacher are locked into a vicious circle. Again, even when punishment does work its effect tends to diminish over time calling for more and more severe measures to control the situation. As we have said before, when this becomes more than pupils can bear they will seek to escape by lying or cheating or will avoid the situation altogether by staying away from the source of conflict by being absent from school.

Generally speaking, the use of negative and punishing sanctions for maintaining rules, or guidelines as some teachers prefer to call them, tends to precipitate conflict situations which are better avoided. In addition, such a system is providing a most unfortunate model for social behaviour. It is teaching, in effect, that might is right. It was for many of these reasons that corporal punishment in schools was abolished and this caused much anxiety to teachers who relied upon it. To use the argument that because society uses such a negative system we have to do the same in school is to miss the point entirely. Society's rule system is to *maintain* the behaviour of adults. School is the place for *teaching* appropriate behaviour to children. In any case, the use of entirely punitive systems of control in society generally might well be questioned.

Most school rules, as in society at large, are framed in negative terms and sanctions are applied to those who disobey the eleventh commandment and allow themselves to be caught. A common characteristic of this system, which most teachers recognise, is that the sanctions apply to only a small minority of the pupil population. The same pupils are found waiting outside the head teacher's room day after day having been sent there, probably by the same teacher. This should cause us to question the effectiveness of the system.

Recognising appropriate behaviour

Our observational survey of teachers designed to measure the extent to which they use positive and negative responses to their pupils' work and behaviour also sampled the pupils' on-task behaviour. As already mentioned, it was found to be 70% on average. This is quite high and yet some teachers were hardly ever referring to this high work rate, concentrating instead on the behaviour of those who were being a nuisance.

It is easy (only too easy, perhaps) to catch children misbehaving in class. So far most of our attention has been directed towards misbehaviour and how we, as teachers, tend to react to it. Now we shall be turning to the other side of the coin, to appropriate behaviour and how we react to that. If we are trying to be more positive we need to be able to recognise appropriate behaviour easily and quickly. In order to do this we need to have definitions of clear, observable behaviours. Teachers or other observers must be able to identify the behaviours in question quickly and readily. If we are observing pupils in the classroom and wish to identify behaviours which could be classed as on-task we might be looking for pupils who are attending to (i.e. looking at) the teacher, pupils raising their hands and waiting to be called upon, pupils volunteering to respond by answering questions or by writing on the blackboard when asked, and so on. We referred to this earlier as pin-pointing, a very important skill for positive teachers.

What we want, as teachers, is for our pupils to improve both in their behavioural patterns and in their work. So what we have to look for is gradual improvement rather than excellence. Children who are not performing very well, whether academically or in terms of their behaviour, are not going to make enormous gains overnight. Spotting the very small increments they will make in the early stages is going to be difficult and will call for the most careful observation. This is why the development of observation skills and especially the precise pin-pointing of behaviours is regarded as being central to Positive Teaching.

An illustration may be appropriate here. At a school in the Inner London Education Authority the teachers decided after much discussion and consultation to give tokens to pupils for improvement in work or conduct. Each teacher had to find ten pupils every week who had improved in some way. To begin with they found it very difficult because they were not used to looking out for small increments of improved performance but after a week or two many of them found themselves dividing the tokens into smaller units because, with practice, they found more and more pupils they wanted to reward for improving. This study indicates that teachers can learn to observe and respond to improved work and behaviour on the part of their pupils and this is the issue that must concern us next.

At this stage it might be profitable for us to consider two linked questions. Why should we, as teachers, be concerned to recognise appropriate academic behaviour? The answer to this is clear. It is our job; to monitor and bring about improvement in their pupils' academic performance is what teachers are paid for. The second question is, perhaps, more controversial. Why should teachers be concerned with recognising and teaching social behaviour? Some teachers might argue that this is not their responsibility. Such teachers expect pupils to behave well and if they do not they blame the pupils themselves or their parents or suggest the sort of reasons we discussed as being unhelpful in Chapter One.

Most teachers would agree, however, that real teaching is about preparing pupils for life in a wider society and that teaching them to behave socially in appropriate ways is an important part of their remit. Good social behaviour, besides being an end in itself by oiling the wheels of social contact, is also an essential prerequisite for most kinds of learning within the group situation. Improved social skill enhances the opportunity for gaining academically, for much is learned through social interactions of all kinds. More crudely, if pupils are being disruptive there is little chance for academic learning to take place however good the curriculum materials or the lesson preparation.

Responding to appropriate behaviour

Being skilful at observing what pupils are doing and what they are achieving is, however, only part of the game. Having observed appropriate behaviour or good learning we have to respond so as to increase the likelihood of that behaviour occurring again. In other words, we have to apply positive reinforcement. This raises two further issues. What is the pupil likely to find rewarding and how shall we deliver it? Most pupils will respond well to social reinforcement and this is relatively easy to dispense. Teachers are very important people to children, especially to the younger ones. Parents will readily testify to this. Many have been amused by the apparent omniscience of the teacher in the child's eyes. In addition, teachers in primary schools have a wealth of materials, activities and practical rewards which most children will go for.

We all use social reinforcement. We all reward those around us at times for their behaviour towards us by the use of quite subtle signals of warmth and approval. We often smile at people in recognition or by way of thanks for something that they have done for us. We make encouraging remarks to people, we thank them for small services and we use all sorts of gestures to indicate approval. We can all learn to increase this behaviour and, by so doing, improve our relationships generally. It should be noted that it is not only what is said that matters. The tone of voice and general demeanour are also important. For example, it is very difficult to make a positive statement without, at the same time, smiling.

All of these comments and gestures except perhaps the smile have to be learned and the reponses to them are also the result of learning. Most of the pupils we meet in school have at least begun to respond to these social signals and with them we have a ready-made language of communication when we want to apply positive reinforcement. However, some of our pupils have not learned to respond so readily to social reinforcement and with them we have an additional problem, but it is still an educational problem and one which is our responsibility. We may have to use more extrinsic rewards initially, a point to which we will return later.

In the last section we were considering behaviour which could be pin-pointed. The teacher might respond by praising pupils for engaging in such pin-pointed behaviours, ignoring minor misde-meanours. It is necessary to stress the need for a professional approach which uses discretion and involves a sense of timing. If you praise a group for working quietly for a time the result may well be that your comment will upset that quiet working pattern. It might be better, perhaps, to wait for a natural break before com-menting. Giving a surprise treat occasionally as a consequence for acceptable behaviour like this has been found to be very effective.

With some pupils, teachers despair of finding anything they have to offer that their pupils will respond to. Nevertheless, we have to persevere because for every person living there are some things or events that they find rewarding. Above all, since everyone prefers some events or happenings to others, we can exploit Grandma's law which says simply that outcomes which are enjoyed may be made dependent upon the completion of others which are less well-liked, with a view to increasing the latter. Grandma says to the young child, "You may have your ice cream when you have eaten all your first course" or, "You can go out to play when you have finished your chores". Similarly, the teacher can offer to allow the class free time or allow individuals to choose a favourite activity once they have completed a set task.

Many teachers have been agreeably surprised when they find out that most pupils respond well to some very simple outcomes that are arranged for them in response to improvement in work or behaviour. There are many ways of delivering rewards through Positive Teaching methods and some of these will be described in later chapters. Children in primary schools respond very well in situations which challenge them to learn and to improve their skills, especially when such improvement is being carefully moni-tored and outcomes are made apparent to them.

For positive reinforcement to be effective it must not only be appropriate but also sincere and is most effective if a variety of forms is used. A teacher may be using a lot of positive utterences but if all he or she ever says is "Good", "Well done" or "OK" then after a while these will lose their effect. If our positive social reinforcement is to be really effective then we have to employ a variety of gestures, statements and actions and suit these to persons and situations as appropriate. This is where our professional skill and our knowledge of our pupils comes into play. We are certainly not suggesting that praise should be scattered willy nilly like confetti regardless of behaviour or effort. In Positive Teaching we make praise and reward contingent upon appropriate work and behaviour. By contingent we mean that praise and reward should follow, and only follow, examples of appropriate behaviour. Positive reinforcement given non-contingently is likely to be counterproductive. For instance, if you congratulate a pupil on a piece of work and he or she knows it was achieved without any real effort, your comment will be wasted and your judgment will be called into question.

When we use social reinforcement we must always try to ensure that it is directed towards the behaviour rather than the person. We want it understood that it is the behaviour that is inappropriate or bad, for example, not the person and the same goes for good behaviour or satisfactory work. Of course, pupils will get satisfaction from the fact that their work or behaviour is worthy of praise but we try to avoid the implication that the person is good or bad *per se*. Our aim is to monitor pupils' behaviour and to respond to it appropriately, not to label them.

Let us consider two questions about positive reinforcement. First, why do you not have to prompt a child to ask for pocket money? The answer is obvious. Money is a reinforcer which, when you receive it, can make all sorts of other good things available to you. All human beings quickly learn to value money so it becomes a very general means of reinforcement for most people, most of the time.

The second question is, why do you have to keep reminding children to wipe their shoes before coming into the house? Obviously wiping your feet has no pay-off. Any mess made is cleaned up by someone else. When do they learn? It is amazing what a difference it makes to this sort of behaviour when young people acquire a place of their own. Then they have to clean up the mess they make or live in squalor (and some, of course, initially do just that!). When they have to find the money to replace worn out or dirty furnishings their response to the importance of simple habits which make things last longer or look better changes because, once again, there is a clear pay-off.

Some social behaviours are followed by powerful positive rein-forcers (such as money) although most (like wiping your feet) are not. Few academic skills are associated with immediately reward-ing outcomes. Part of the task of teachers (and parents), as educators, is to provide young people with extrinsic positive rein-forcement until the time when the behaviour will be maintained by intrinsic reinforcement. If you read this book and find it satisfying a need so that you feel that you have learned something from it and can now begin to do your job with greater confidence, then nobody will need to praise you for reading it. The reward is intrinsic, built into the task itself. The same applies to a recipe that you manage to follow successfully.

Those of our pupils who succeed in their academic work and in their social and sporting life in school will be receiving a great deal of intrinsic satisfaction from all these activities. But what about those who are less successful? They are getting few rewards and we have to structure a situation in which we provide extrinsic reward systems for them until they, too, begin to enjoy the intrinsic rewards which come from being successful and accepted by those around them. For some, starting a long way back in the race, this is going to be a lengthy process but it is all part of our remit as teachers. Positive teachers do not go in for labelling this or that pupil as remedial or hyperactive and then assume that nothing can be done. They do not indulge in such explanatory fictions but prefer, instead, to observe carefully, find some positive elements in the pupil's behaviour and to work to increase those. As soon as it can be arranged for the pupil to receive some reward for behaviour which is profitable for him or her, for the other pupils or the teacher we are on the way to improvement. One of the chief difficulties is to find something that is likely to be rewarding for pupils who have found very few rewards in the system so far. One event to which most of them will respond favourably is the understanding and acceptance that somebody is interested in their problem and ready to offer practical help. The various ways in which this can be achieved will be discussed more fully in Chapters Four and Five.

Nothing that has been written so far is meant to give the impression that it is easy to be a positive teacher. If the effects of the approach are to be maximised then we need to use our imagination, initiative and resourcefulness to the full. Positive Teaching is no panacea. It is not to be thought of as an ointment that can be rubbed on and left to do the job. To achieve effective classroom management by means of Positive Teaching teachers have to monitor their own behaviour. In order to improve our skill in observing and responding to pupils we have to practise.

We need to find times when we are teaching, and it must be admitted that teaching is a task which takes almost all of our energy and concentration, when we can observe our pupils and ourselves. For this we need a schedule of some kind on which we have written a clear definition of what we are looking for and some simple system for recording events. Alternatively, a tally-counter, a mechanical device which records numbers successively as it is pressed, may be found useful. These can be bought at some stationers but are, unfortunately, rather expensive. Some hand calculators can be programmed to do the same thing. Another way is to arrange with a colleague to observe you in action and then to reciprocate. Or you could record yourself teaching. Either of these methods will give you an indication of how good you are at using positive and negative responding effectively. We will return to this issue in Chapter Four. Descriptions of simple observation schedules and how teachers can monitor their own behaviour may be found in our earlier book, *Positive Teaching: the behavioural approach*.

To sum up, our research shows that teachers can be positive, encouraging and supportive of pupils' academic efforts but when it comes to their classroom behaviour the emphasis appears to be almost overwhelmingly negative. The continual litany of reprimands we hear on entering some classes is almost always an attempt to deal with disruptive classroom behaviours. The focus is on detecting and dealing with inappropriate behaviour rather than recognising and rewarding appropriate behaviour. Very rarely are attempts made to encourage more appropriate forms of classroom behaviour. Similarly, the systems which schools develop for maintaining discipline are structured so as to punish transgressions rather than to encourage more responsible behaviour. Teachers and schools attempting to apply Positive Teaching techniques will have to engineer changes in systems and practices. The means for bringing about changes in pupils' behaviour and their academic standards are available. What teachers have to decide is whether it is worth the effort.

Further reading

A more detailed account of the principles and procedures of Positive Teaching is given in our earlier work:

Wheldall, K. and Merrett, F. (1984). *Positive Teaching: the behavioural approach.* London: Allen & Unwin, reprinted 1989 by Positive Products, Birmingham.

The application of Positive Teaching methods to encourage academic learning is detailed in:

Wheldall, K. and Glynn, T. (1989). *Effective Classroom Learning: a behavioural interactionist approach to teaching.* Oxford: Basil Blackwell.

Our observational study of primary school teachers' use of praise and reprimands is reported fully in:

Merrett, F. and Wheldall, K. (1987). Natural rates of teacher approval and disapproval in British primary and middle school classrooms. *British Journal of Educational Psychology, 57,* 95-103.

Chapter Three
SETTING THE CLASSROOM
CONTEXT

Most teachers will have noticed how the behaviour of a class can vary depending on who is teaching them and where they are being taught. Being with a certain teacher or even in that teacher's room may be the cue for unruly behaviour because pupils have learned that they can get away with such behaviour with that particular teacher in that situation. With another teacher and in a different room few of the same group of children would dare even to breathe too loudly having expectations of the second teacher's likely response to any such behaviour, however harmless. Similarly, academic lessons, held by necessity in an unfamiliar room may lead to more disruptive behaviour than when held in the usual classroom.

As we have said, it is not sufficient to attempt to explain learning simply in terms of behaviours and reinforcers as we have done so far. As well as considering what happens after a behaviour occurs (the consequence) we should also consider what happened just before the behaviour occurred and the context in which it occurred (the antecedents). As already mentioned in Chapter One, antecedent events also have great power to influence behaviour.

Antecedents can serve to prompt certain behaviours. Consider the situation when a teacher leaves the room and the class is left alone. For some classes this may have become a cue for noisy, disruptive behaviour since there is no-one present to reprimand the pupils. When the teacher returns, the noisy disruptive behaviour will cease. We can see here how specific antecedent conditions influence particular behaviours in association with certain consequences.

Let us take another example which highlights how this might occur. The teacher asks Jenny a question in class (antecedent),

Jenny gives a silly answer (behaviour) and her classmates laugh (consequence). Since this laughter is probably rewarding for her we may expect Jenny to produce silly answers on similar occasions subsequently. She will be less likely to do so, however, when her classmates are not there. The presence of classroom peers has become a cue for her inappropriate behaviour. This example underlines the need to consider the context in which behaviours occur and demonstrates how some antecedents develop their power to influence behaviour.

Within the classroom environment it is known that a wide range of antecedent events will influence behaviour and they do this in at least two basic ways. First, there are those antecedent conditions which provide constraints or opportunities for behaviour. We are thinking here of factors such as seating arrangements or the presence or absence of particular materials or curriculum aids or of other people. Secondly, there are antecedent conditions which have acquired power over certain behaviours by association with rewarding or punishing circumstances, as we have shown above. Antecedents encompass a variety of features of the environment which may influence pupils' behaviour. These features range from specific actions by a teacher or another pupil to more global aspects of the environment such as heating and lighting levels, the arrangement of furniture and materials and the management of classroom seating.

This key principle of Positive Teaching, that children's behaviour can be greatly influenced by antecedent contextual factors, appears to be little appreciated and greatly under-utilised in classroom teaching. Positive teachers should identify which particular antecedents in their classrooms have clear effects on children's learning. They can then work to manipulate some of these, for most are under their direct control, to bring about changes in the climate of the classroom. When teachers make effective use of antecedent events to encourage appropriate behaviour they have more time to spend on teaching and instruction.

The importance of curriculum issues

Before embarking upon discussion of the importance of the various key antecedents in more detail it is necessary to establish one fact of vital importance about the learning/teaching situation. The curriculum materials with which the teacher seeks to engage the attention of his or her pupils must be appropriate. They must be appropriate in terms of what the pupils know already and the skills they have at their disposal. They must relate to the curriculum elements about to be tackled and, above all, they must present a challenge and be of interest to the pupils. We have to accept that not all learning can be of compelling interest and fascination all of the time. Mastery of some skills, techniques and procedures calls for prolonged practice and some of this practice can be quite boring and, for the time being, apparently fruitless. But life and work are like that and children have to learn to be tolerant of some learning and work processes, elements of which are not immediately exciting.

Nevertheless, it is possible to leaven the lump and most of what pupils do in school should appeal, should be exciting and should have obvious value for them, even if not in the immediate future. If the curriculum they are led to follow is without some excitement, some challenge, some enjoyment and if it does not aim eventually at the pupils' ultimate and lasting good, it cannot be called educational and has no place in the school or the classroom. Her Majesty's Inspectorate have called attention more than once to the importance of matching the content of the curriculum to the needs of pupils. If we are serious about equality of opportunity we must recognise the need for a curriculum appropriate for all our pupils whatever their cultural or social background. We will not labour this point further here, but it is fundamental to all that follows.

What we are *not* endorsing is that old cliche, so well-loved by some college lecturers, that provided you have prepared your lesson properly you will have no discipline problems. Most teachers will know from bitter experience that some classes or pupils will be troublesome regardless of the amount of time, creativity and energy spent in preparing exciting and relevant lessons. On the other hand, it is only fair to add that some pupil misbehaviour may be perceived as a legitimate protest against tedious lessons on topics of little relevance presented in a pedestrian and boring manner.

Quiet reading periods are a case in point. A widely agreed goal of primary education is to foster in pupils an affinity for books and reading. Consequently, once some of the basic skills of reading have been mastered, many teachers timetable quiet reading periods for their pupils, often on a daily basis, in an attempt to encourage reading for its own sake. Meanwhile, teachers often busy themselves by engaging in classroom chores such as pinning up work, marking books, writing on the blackboard or, more commonly, by hearing individual children read aloud. This can be distracting for the silent readers and may also become a cue for children to chat among themselves instead of reading. Quiet reading is thus not perceived to be an important or worthwhile activity.

Teachers can demonstrate the importance of reading as a recreational activity by modelling the desired behaviour of quiet reading. This is sometimes referred to as USSR or Uninterrupted Sustained Silent Reading. We recently carried out several studies demonstrating that teacher modelling of appropriate reading behaviour during USSR sessions consistently leads to marked increases in the amount of time pupils spend actually reading.

The studies were undertaken in two primary schools with third- and fourth-year junior classes. In all four classes silent reading sessions were held frequently but the teachers typically used these times to listen to individual readers or to carry out other tasks in the classroom. During these experiments, at the start of all sessions, the teachers announced clearly that it was to be a quiet reading time and the children were to read their own books. Whilst USSR was in operation and the teachers were modelling reading, the children were informed that it was to be a quiet reading time, that the teacher had his or her own book to read which was very interesting and did not want to be disturbed. The teacher then sat reading the book in a prominent position. Observation sessions lasted for the first fifteen minutes of each daily reading session of fifteen to twenty minutes duration and the amount of time the children spent reading quietly was recorded.

The first study, which lasted six weeks, involved a class of 23 ten to eleven-year olds. During the initial sessions, time spent reading averaged 50% but this figure rose to a mean of 73% during the first USSR phase when the teacher modelled silent reading. This level dropped back to 56% when USSR was discontinued and rose again to 82% when it was reintroduced. In other words, USSR led to around 25% increases in time spent reading. In a second, bigger study with three third- and fourth-year classes, the results were equally clear. In all three classes the amount of time spent actually reading during USSR sessions was, on average, between 20% and 30% higher than usual. We also looked at the number of individual pupils whose behaviour was influenced by teacher modelling of silent reading. Further data were collected from ten children and we found that eight of them had clearly increased the amount of time they spent quietly reading during USSR sessions.

This series of studies demonstrates the effectiveness of USSR in encouraging quiet recreational reading and, more generally, how teacher behaviour is an important antecedent for pupil behaviour. The teachers involved in these studies said that their pupils were now reading more books than they usually did. This was partly a result of them having more regular reading sessions but also because they spent more time actually reading during the USSR sessions. The ways in which we deliver the curriculum are clearly important antecedents for behaviour as these studies show.

Arranging the classroom

We now turn to a consideration of the ecology of the classroom. It has been demonstrated quite clearly that the conditions under which people work affects their output. If they are cold, hungry, unduly worried or stressed they cannot perform up to their usual standard. Likewise, if pupils cannot hear what the teacher is saying because he or she is too far away or is speaking too softly or with an unfamiliar accent they will soon lose the sense of what is going on and will cease to attend. Sometimes children are hindered in following the interaction because they cannot see clearly what is being demonstrated on the blackboard. All of these are very obvious reasons for pupils' difficulties and most of them are under the direct and easy control of the teacher. However, the teacher must be aware of them, be vigilant to notice them and respond to remove them whenever possible. Some teachers, especially those who are new to the profession, are so concerned with other matters of presentation or procedure that they are not aware of such problems and fail to see how they can be avoided.

Another source of problems is movement in the classroom. Sometimes it is necessary and desirable for pupils to move about in the classroom in order to gain access to equipment, to refer to charts, dictionaries or other resource materials. Indeed, there are times when we actually set out to programme and encourage such activities in, for example, science lessons or CDT. Therefore, it must be made possible for them to do so easily and efficiently without disturbing others. In addition, they have to know where the materials they need are to be found, what the procedures are for gaining permission to use them (if this is thought to be necessary) and they have to have access to proper routeways so they have unhindered passage. All of this calls for careful planning in the arrangement of furniture and of the storage facilities for the convenience of the group. In addition, it underlines the need for agreed procedures for giving out and collecting in (and checking) equipment. Routines for such basic administrative procedures are absolutely essential for a well-run classroom and experienced, successful teachers know that they can reduce much of the daily stress.

The organisation of seating arrangements is another area which needs attention in some classrooms. In some situations it is a good idea to allow pupils to choose where they sit. In others it can be a recipe for disaster. There is no doubt at all that by manipulating seating arrangements changes can be brought about in the behaviour of pupils. Most teachers will be aware that in some classes a certain group of pupils will seek seats (usually at the back of the room) in order to carry on certain ploys which they, the teachers, find annoying or disruptive to the rest of the class. By insisting that such pupils occupy seats designated by themselves, teachers may be able to control the situation. Again, pupils who are constantly off-task or interfering with the work of others around them can often be brought into line by moving them to sit nearer the teacher or away from peers who are reinforcing their behaviour with attention.

These examples are anecdotal but more formal experiments have been carried out to show that such strategies are based upon sound principles. We have been able to show that simple manipulation of seating arrangements between pupils sitting in rows or around tables in top junior classes can bring about quite large changes in the pupils' on-task behaviour.

Since the practice was strongly commended in the Plowden Report, children in most primary classes in this country sit around tables in groups of four, five or six. The justification for this was that children can learn from each other through discussion and co-operation. However, for this to stand any chance of success the nature of the work set must be a group activity requiring collaboration. The reality is that whilst seating may have changed, the work demands have not. Much of the work set is still individually based, children being expected to work on their own, using work cards, for example. As a consequence, much of the talk in table groups tends to be chatter not related to the work in hand. There is a mis-match between the nature of the tasks set and the seating arrangements leading to less time spent on-task and less work being completed.

We carried out parallel studies in two junior schools with classes of 10 to 11 year-old children. One class consisted of 28 boys and girls of mixed ability attending a school in an urban residential area whereas the other consisted of 25 similar children from a school on a council housing estate. In both classes the children normally sat around tables in groups.

The children in both classes were initially observed for two weeks (ten days) in their normal seating arrangements around tables. An observation schedule was employed to obtain estimates of on-task behaviour. This was defined as doing what the teacher had asked, i.e. pupils looking at and listening to her when she was talking to them or looking at their books or work cards when they were required to complete set work, only being out of their seats with the teacher's permission and so on.

After observing the class for two weeks sitting around tables the desks/tables were moved into rows without comment from the teacher and the children were observed for a further two weeks using the same procedure. Finally, the desks were moved back to their original positions, again without comment, for a further two weeks of observation. This time there were complaints from the children as some of them said they preferred sitting in rows.

In both classes on-task behaviour rose by around 15% overall when the children were placed in rows and fell by nearly as much when they returned to sitting around tables. Looking at individual children, the most marked improvements (over 30%) occurred for those whose on-task behaviour had previously been very low. As we might expect, the effect was less in the case of those with high initial on-task behaviour.

Subsequent studies have replicated these findings many times and have also shown that on-task behaviour remains high even after several weeks of sitting in rows. Moreover, we have shown that the quantity and the quality of work produced is greater when children are seated in rows. Let us emphasise immediately, however, that we are not advocating a back to rows movement for all children for all work. What we are saying is that teachers should *vary* the seating arrangements to suit the task in hand.

Most of us would advocate that, ideally, children should be given as much choice as possible as to where they sit and with whom. In classrooms arranged in table groups this almost inevitably results in girls and boys being seated around separate tables. Similarly, in classes where children sit in rows children of the same sex prefer to sit next to each other. Teachers sometimes claim, however, that one of the most effective ways of curbing the disruptive behaviour of children, particularly boys, is to sit them next to a member of the opposite sex. The aim of the following study was to determine whether mixed-sex seating does in fact, produce such clear effects, in terms of changes in on-task behaviour.

The study was carried out with two classes in a junior school in an inner-city area. One class consisted of 31 mixed ability children (16 boys, 15 girls) aged 9 to 10 years and the other comprised 25 similar 10 to 11 year-old children (13 boys and 12 girls). Both class teachers were female.

In the younger class, the children were seated around six groups of tables. Three of the groups of tables were occupied solely by girls, the other three by boys. During the intervention phase of the study, the boys and girls were mixed so that boys and girls were now sitting next to each other. In the other class, the children were seated at conventional double desks, not tables. The desks were arranged in three rows and all of the children usually sat next to a member of the opposite sex. During the intervention period, girls and boys in each row changed places so that they were now sitting by a member of the same sex.

Again, in this study the two classes were first observed for two weeks in their usual seating conditions followed by a two-week intervention phase. Observations carried out under the changed seating conditions were then followed by two more weeks of observation with children back in their usual seats. The results clearly showed that on-task behaviour in the older class, seated in rows, decreased (by 15%) when the children of the same sex sat together. In the younger class, seated in groups, on-task behaviour increased (by about 15%) when the normal same-sex seating was changed in favour of mixed-sex seating. The conclusion to be drawn is that mixed-sex seating produces the highest pupil on-task levels. Similarly, disruptive behaviour in both classes was at its lowest when boys and girls sat together. What also emerged clearly from the results was that children with the lowest on-task study levels were most positively affected by the change from mixed to same-sex seating.

We are not necessarily advocating any particular type of seating arrangement, although there are some occasions when control of seating can be used to good effect; to establish some measure of control with an unruly class, for example. What we would emphasise, once again, is the importance of *flexibility*; of matching the seating arrangements to the task in hand. More generally, positive teachers seek to optimise the classroom environment so as to encourage appropriate behaviour and effective learning.

Ensuring the smooth flow of the lesson

Once we have made sure that the subject matter is appropriate for the pupils and that the ecological factors in the classroom setting are right it is then important to ensure that the lesson proceeds smoothly. When a group of pupils is well-organised so that each knows what has to be done and in what order, there is less danger that things will get out of hand. Some of the confusion and disruption we observe in classrooms stems from the fact that some of the pupils cannot cope for one reason or another or that they have completed their work quickly and do not know what else to occupy themselves with.

First and foremost, teachers must ensure that their pupils understand clearly the nature of the task that has been set. If instructions are given verbally the teacher must be sure that all have heard them clearly and understand. In order to find out if this is the case the teacher can ask one of the pupils to recount the instructions. Once a teacher gets to know his or her pupils it is easy to pick pupils who are less likely to attend to instructions. Once we feel sure that such pupils have got the full message we can have confidence that most of the others will also. Generally speaking, it is best if teachers refrain from repeating their instructions as this teaches pupils that they do not have to listen the first time instructions are given out since they will shortly be repeated. It is always better to have another student repeat instructions for the rest, if this proves to be necessary.

Once instructions have been given they have to be remembered and another opportunity for misunderstanding or interruption of the learning process can occur when pupils, having made a good start, then fail to recall what they have to do next. One way of overcoming this problem is to divide the process into small sections and to give directions for each separately as they are completed. This can give rise to other problems, however, as all pupils will not proceed at the same pace, but if the teacher is moving round the group in order to keep an eye on the progress being made, it can be a useful device. If the learning process or the sequence of tasks is complicated it is probably best if the instructions are given in written form, perhaps on a blackboard or flipchart, so that reference to this can be made at any juncture for additional guidance. This is where worksheets come into their own. Where instructions are complicated, or if pupils are not good readers, they probably need to be taken through the script before being asked to make a start. In these cases diagrams, especially flow diagrams, may be a useful aid.

It will probably be helpful if details of equipment or other necessary materials are also listed on worksheets. It was mentioned above that procedures for obtaining equipment are an important factor in classroom management. Failure on the part of the pupils to have the necessary equipment is a frequent cause of interruption to the smooth flow of a lesson. If teachers can arrange for pupils to be warned, in advance, of any extra equipment they will need for certain lessons this is less likely to happen. Teachers should always ensure that equipment commonly needed for work in their classrooms is routinely available and have spares like ready-sharpened pencils and extra pens, rulers and erasers to hand. This may sound obvious and as though we are trying to teach grandmothers to suck eggs but, as the Elton Report makes clear, it is surprising how often such elementary procedures are not observed.

If the subject matter to be taught involves equipment that is not used every day the teacher will do well to think through carefully how it is to be made available. Perhaps it is best if the material is placed ready for use before the lesson begins. In some circumstances, however, this can be counter-productive. If prior explanation is necessary then the presence of new or unfamiliar equipment within easy reach may be difficult for some pupils to resist and they may begin to play with it. In such cases it is necessary to decide at which point the introduction of the equipment is going to be most useful and to consider carefully the best method of distribution. These issues are not trivial in terms of classroom management and can make the difference between the success and failure of otherwise carefully prepared lessons. In some lessons changes of classroom seating are necessary. In such cases it is well worthwhile to spend time at the beginning of the school year practising the correct procedures for altering the seating arrangements or for obtaining equipment.

The interventions described below were carried out with two groups of younger boys and girls in a junior school by two teachers each working with her own class. Neither class was particularly difficult to handle. These interventions were concerned with small routine matters which cause teachers' nerves to fray and can lead to a great deal of negative 'nagging' behaviour on the teacher's part.

The aim of the first study was to get all the children to remember their pencils for both morning and afternoon sessions. The teacher provided a large sheet of paper with a race track drawn on it. This was pinned up on the wall so that everyone could see it. She also provided a number of large pictures of cars that could be fixed on to the track with Blu-Tack. At the beginning of each session the teacher asked the children to show their pencils. If everyone in the class had his or her pencil then one car was put on the track for the pencil rally. To begin with, as soon as there were five cars on the track every child received a sweet. Later, ten cars were necessary to earn the same reward. The same basic idea was applied by the teacher to the bringing of reading books to the classroom. In this case, however, instead of checking at the beginning of the lesson she would make her check at random times when the children were unprepared.

Many of the children from this class also seemed to forget their P.E. clothing. The teacher devised a P.E. ladder, which was a chart placed on the wall in the form of a ladder. There were eight steps, one for each letter of the phrase P.E. ladder. Each of these letters was covered by a piece of paper held in place by Blu-Tack. Every time all the class remembered their P.E. kit the teacher removed one of the pieces of paper, disclosing the letter underneath. When all the letters had been uncovered the reward was a free P.E. lesson in which the children were allowed to choose the activities. This proved to be a very popular reward which the children were prepared to strive for, showing once again that the simplest schemes can be very effective with children when teachers are imaginative.

The third study was carried out by another teacher. The children at this school were encouraged to take their reading books home but some were not very good about bringing them back again the next morning. Every day two or three children from this class, on average, would forget to bring their books. In order to solve this problem the teacher took a sheet of wrapping paper which had a complete picture on one side of it. This she cut into five unequal and irregular polygons. Each morning a check was made and if all the children had brought their books back one child was allowed to paste up one part of the picture on to a framework. When the picture was complete with all five pieces in position the children enjoyed a reward, usually a sweet each.

In each of these studies there was an immediate improvement in the number of children remembering their pencils, their P.E. equipment or their reading books. There was not a 100% response, of course, but then we are not trying to produce saints. In the case of the third study, for example, on only one or two occasions per week would a child fail to come to school with his or her book. This was a great improvement and a situation that was much easier to cope with.

These three simple devices show how effective use can be made of Positive Teaching methods by an imaginative teacher and with little expenditure of effort. They also show how children tend to respond to the approach. Each of these studies has the same basic features: first, a clearly defined behaviour to be observed and counted, second a clear visual record for the children which serves as a prompt or antecedent, and, third, a clear and effective reward.

Some teachers might object to giving sweets as rewards on health grounds and we would agree. A whole range of other suitable rewards could be substituted for sweets in these studies.

In a well-ordered classroom it is necessary also to have routines for the pupils to follow when they need help. Most teachers will ask their pupils to raise their hands if they want to contribute to discussion or need help and this works well enough in most instances. Nevertheless, there are drawbacks to this procedure because it means that when several pupils are seeking help at the same time, some may be kept waiting for quite long periods with nothing to do. As mentioned above, delays which cause interruption to the smooth flow of the lesson are prone to lead to problems in classroom management and should be avoided if at all possible. Another common device is to invite pupils who have problems to come to the teacher sitting at his or her desk. This, too, can work well but unless care is taken to prevent it, may lead to long queues building up. Standing in a queue provides opportunities for all sorts of misbehaviour.

We carried out an observational study of children waiting for teacher attention. A sample of twenty British female infant school teachers and their classes was observed, selected to include a range of catchment areas and types of school. Each class teacher agreed to have an observer present for four 30 minute sessions. Data were collected by scanning the class at one-minute intervals and counting the number of boys and girls (separately) waiting for attention from the teacher and whether they were sitting with a hand raised or queuing at the teacher's desk. Since the numerical count at each timed interval would not give any indication of the waiting time for any single child, a system of timing individual children by stop watch was also incorporated.

On average, nearly three children (varying from zero to 21) were observed to be waiting at any one time, in classes of approximately thirty children. Half of the teachers usually had fewer than two children waiting but one-fifth of teachers had four or more children, on average, waiting for attention at any one time. There was very little difference between the mean numbers of boys and girls waiting but the mean number of children waiting rose as the lesson progressed. The mean length of time spent waiting was about one and a half minutes but this was highly variable, ranging from zero (when children received immediate attention) to over 13 minutes. This should be appreciated in the context of the length of the observation period, 30 minutes.

Queuing proved to be more efficient than the hands up system of signalling, in terms of the length of time children had to wait for teacher attention, but hands up may be preferable from a classroom management point of view, since it involves more teacher movement around the room. Teachers who move systematically from table to table are better able to monitor children's work. One possibility is to use a mobile queue system, where the teacher moves from table to table, and children needing help queue and move with him or her. This method incorporates the best feature of the queuing procedure (a shorter waiting time for children), whilst at the same time allowing the teacher to monitor the work of individuals or groups of children. This study illustrates, yet again, the importance of antecedent events (in this case procedures for seeking help) in classroom behaviour management.

The following study continues this theme and demonstrates how further consideration of appropriate antecedents can prove helpful in managing waiting time. This involved helping children to learn to be more independent in solving their own problems, with less teacher attention. Four junior classes including children aged from 7 to 11 years were observed once per week during mathematics lessons. A modified version of the OPTIC schedule, described earlier, was employed to record pupil on-task and teacher behaviours together with measures of the amount of on-task behaviour (i.e. behaving appropriately) among the pupils queuing. The number of pupils queuing for teacher attention at any one time was also sampled. Preliminary observations were made over four weeks with two classes and over five weeks with the other two and showed, as expected, that in all four classes pupils spent significant amounts of time waiting for attention.

Consequently, the following strategy was employed. With the aid of simple flow charts, children were shown what to do when they were stuck and needed help from the teacher with their maths problems. When about to seek help they were asked first to pause to see whether they could help themselves by re-reading the question or problem. If this did not prove to be helpful they were asked to look back at the previous question to see if this yielded any clues. If this did not prove helpful they were asked to miss out that problem and to try the next but to go back and try the problem they had missed out, again, later. If they still needed help they were invited to try (quietly) asking their neighbour for assistance. Finally, if all these avenues had been explored without success they were allowed to seek help from their teacher, who was instructed to praise them for trying out the independent strategies.

All four classes responded well to this idea and considerable improvements were evident when the classes were observed for a further three or four weeks. On average, on-task behaviour in the four classes increased from 83% to 96% but, more importantly, average waiting time dropped from 16% to 5%. This meant that, on average, time spent actually working (academically engaged) increased from 68% to 91%. The number of children waiting for attention at any one time dropped from over three, on average, to one. An interesting concomitant of this was that the teachers increased the amount of praise they gave and decreased their use of reprimands. These very welcome, positive effects were brought about using a relatively simple strategy based mainly on the use of effective antecedents to encourage more independent behaviour in the children.

It will readily be seen that having too many pupils not knowing what to do next, or how to proceed, is closely linked to the discussion earlier about the appropriateness of the task. Nevertheless, there will be occasions when many of the pupils are having difficulty. On such occasions it will often be found that they share a common problem or that there is a common misunderstanding. In such cases it will be necessary to stop the lesson briefly and to explain a way around the problem for the whole or part of the class. In lessons where there are several procedures or several sections to be attempted it is possible to accustom pupils to register the fact that they need help and then to turn to another section they can cope with, whilst they are waiting for the teacher to attend to them.

It will be appreciated that much of the discussion so far in this section has been to ensure that the lesson, once begun, should flow smoothly giving little opportunity for undesirable or disruptive behaviour. Pupils who have plenty to occupy their attention, work which they find absorbing and which is within their capacities, will usually be prepared to get on with it and will have little time or opportunity for upsetting the rest of the group.

There is one other situation which can give rise to problems of classroom management and that is when pupils finish the work which has been set and do not know what to do next. Once again, this occurrence can be the result of poor planning or of poor instruction about what has to be done. In well-ordered classrooms the teacher will always be aware of the necessity for pupils to have work to do when for one reason or another they have completed the task or tasks which have been set for the day or the period. In most primary school classes children are involved in project or topic work for some of the school day. Permission to get on with this sort of work or to engage in reading will usually be welcomed by most pupils and this will allow the teacher to benefit from the operation of Grandma's law as explained in Chapter Two. In other words, a task which is more acceptable is made contingent upon first completing one which is less agreeable.

The effectiveness of using different task requirements to bring about a change in behaviour is demonstrated in the following example. This study was carried out with a vertically grouped class of third and fourth year juniors in a school situated in the middle of a council estate in the West Midlands. The 28 children in the class, following a term with an inexperienced temporary teacher, had fallen into bad habits in certain situations and the regular class teacher was looking for methods to eliminate these. The main problem occurred during the morning registration period when the children had previously been expected to pick up a book and read.

A baseline was obtained by making observations of on-task behaviour (defined as reading silently whilst each child was occupying his or her own seat) at 9.05 a.m. each day for seven working days. This time was chosen because it was the mid-point between children coming into the classroom and the class going to assembly. These baseline data confirmed that very few children were on-task. The teacher decided to change the antecedent conditions by introducing a new concept of on-task behaviour and to offer encouragement through the giving of house points.

The children were asked to produce their own individual topic booklets based on the class topic which was "Journeys". The necessary materials and reference books were readily available and the children were free to choose their own subjects for their booklets. The targeted behaviour for the intervention was "working purposefully on own topic booklet" and at the end of each week when house points were totalled for the school, each child who had worked well during the registration periods received a house point. The teacher also promised that the best three booklets would receive a small prize at the end of term.

The effect of this policy was felt immediately. The number of children on-task increased from a mean level of 6 to about 20. The atmosphere in the classroom was greatly improved, the registration period became more purposeful and many house points were awarded. The teacher reported that noise levels were much reduced once the intervention began and that many children sought chances to continue their booklets at times other than the registration period. This intervention might have been even more effective had the children been given a free choice of topic but that could have created problems in the supply of books. The intervention was effective over the four weeks for which it ran but it is likely that children would need a change of project every so often in order to maintain interest.

Setting effective classroom rules

Another major set of antecedents which influence classroom behaviour are classroom rules. All social groups have rules and school classes are no exception to this. In many social situations the rules are implicit and we learn to abide by and accept these implied rules because to do so oils the wheels of social contact. If we voluntarily join a group of other people for some common purpose then we have an incentive for learning their rules. But school classes are artificial groupings where the members are arbitrarily selected for a particular purpose, that of instruction and learning together. The rules are often implicit or unclear and are generally imposed by teachers. Pupils have to learn to accommodate to them as far as they are able but this calls for interpretation on their part. This can result in unfortunate outcomes for some pupils. They may adopt strategies which seem to them to conform to what they believe the teacher expects but which are, in fact, unproductive for learning.

From a Positive Teaching perspective we would suggest that rules are important antecedents in schools and in classes and that they should be made explicit. Positive teachers will arrive at a set of rules not by imposing them but through negotiation with their pupils. Even quite young children are capable of understanding how a set of reasonable rules can make the classroom climate more acceptable and how they can make life easier and more pleasant for all. If pupils are asked to suggest rules they will probably come up with some very negative suggestions at first, to be supported by equally negative sanctions. This is not what we have in mind, however. We have to accept their suggestions and then encourage the pupils to translate them into a more positive form.

There are three key criteria for effective classroom rules. First, we believe that classroom rules should be positively phrased specifying appropriate behaviour rather than prohibiting inappropriate behaviour. Secondly, they should be specific and objective so that the situation and the behaviour are clearly defined, allowing both teacher and pupils to know when the rules are being kept. Finally, classroom rules should be practical. There is no point in asking for the impossible and we find that the inclusion of the word *try* in rules makes them more acceptable and practicable.

If a teacher says that there is to be no talking then he or she has to be alert to catch the first pupil to break the rule and do something about it otherwise his or her authority will be under threat. There is a danger that pupils may learn that this teacher makes rule statements but does not enforce them. On the other hand if the teacher negotiates rules such as, "We try to work quietly" then he or she can concentrate on appropriate behaviour and pay attention to pupils who are keeping the rules. Positive rules help us to avoid conflict.

Some people might argue that because the rules of society are framed in the form of "Thou shalt not" and are supported by sanctions of one sort or another, schools should maintain the same structure. However, it must be appreciated that society's rules are meant to maintain the behaviour of adults whereas in school we have a different objective, namely the teaching of new behaviours to a fresh generation and this confronts us with quite different problems. The positive teacher then will seek to negotiate through discussion with his or her pupils a set of rules which are phrased positively, which are seen to be reasonable and which pupils believe they can keep. These rules should be few in number (not more than three or four) should be written on a notice and displayed prominently. In one infant class where rules were negotiated in this way the children spontaneously signed their names at the bottom of the notice and proudly showed "our rules" to visitors to the classroom. In nursery or reception classes photographs of children engaged in appropriate behaviour might be used to illustrate the class rules.

When pupils are working with a set of imposed and negative rules it is usual for those in control to call attention to the rules when they have been broken. A child will be punished and reminded at the same time that he or she has broken a stated rule. When positive rules are negotiated we write them down so that they may be referred to at suitable times (the beginning of the day, perhaps) to remind those who have agreed to them what we are striving to do for the comfort and convenience of all. Because their number is few they do not have to remain the same for ever. In fact, once pupils have become accustomed to keeping a rule, that rule may be dropped and another can take its place. For instance, let us assume that one of the original rules was to raise your hand and wait to be asked if you want to answer a question. After a while this may become second nature to the members of the group and may be replaced by a rule dealing with more polite ways of interacting with one's neighbours, telling the pupils that this is because they are "so good at putting up their hands now". As we have said, it has been found that to use the word *try* in defining the rules is useful because one can still be congratulated for trying even when one has not succeeded. We will return to the important issue of classroom rules in Chapter Five.

So far what has been discussed has related to the classroom but pupils are subject also to another rule system which is general to the school. It is important that this, too, should be positive in its outlook but this state of affairs can only be brought about by concerted action of the whole staff. We have found that when the whole staff of a school have followed a course in Positive Teaching they will frequently agree to apply the same principles about rule making to the school as a whole. In a Birmingham inner-ring primary school, rules for the whole school were negotiated with all children from nursery to top juniors in the context of a school-wide project about rules. This tends to give a positive flavour to the ethos and feel of the whole community. It is self-evident that if people feel that they have had some say in what the rules are to be, they will be better motivated to keep them and this should apply to pupils in school also. If they are to learn how a rule system (designed to teach acceptable behaviour and democratically arrived at) is to work, what better model could they have than that of their own school?

Further reading

The study on teacher modelling of reading is reported in:

Wheldall, K. and Entwistle, J. (1988). Back in the USSR: the effect of teacher modelling of silent reading on pupils' reading behaviour in the primary school classroom. *Educational Psychology, 8,* 51-66.

Studies on classroom seating arrangements are reported in:

Wheldall, K., Morris, M., Vaughan, P. and Ng, Y.Y. (1981). Rows versus tables: an example of the use of behavioural ecology in two classes of eleven year-old children. *Educational Psychology, 1,* 171-184.

Wheldall, K. and Olds, P. (1987). Of sex and seating: the effects of mixed and same-sex seating arrangements in junior school classrooms. *New Zealand Journal of Educational Studies, 22,* 71-85.

A chapter detailing our research on classroom seating arrangements is included in:

Wheldall, K. and Glynn, T. (1989). *Effective Classroom Learning: a behavioural interactionist approach to teaching.* Oxford: Basil Blackwell.

Studies on ensuring the smooth flow of the lesson are reported in:

Merrett, F. (1986). *Encouragement Works Better Than Punishment* (second edition). Birmingham: Positive Products.

The study on time spent waiting for teacher attention is reported in:

West, C. and Wheldall, K. (1989). Waiting for teacher: the frequency and duration of times children spend waiting for teacher attention in infant school classrooms. *British Educational Research Journal, 15,* 205-216.

Chapter Four
ENHANCING PRAISE AND REPRIMANDS

In his famous essay *On Education,* the seventeenth-century phi-
losopher, John Locke wrote, "Esteem and disgrace are, of all
others, the most powerful incentives to the mind, when once it is
brought to relish them". Locke regarded the achievement of this as
"the great secret of education". He continued,

> Children (earlier perhaps than we think) are very sensible of
> praise and commendation. They find a pleasure in being esteemed
> and valued, especially by their parents, and those whom they
> depend on.

Locke's comments on praise, first aired over 300 years ago, may
sound painfully obvious to many teachers but it is our contention
that the lesson has still to be learned.

Most teachers would agree that to use encouragement and approval is more effective than to rely upon negative procedures with
their pupils. A key principle of Positive Teaching is finding out
what pupils will respond to or go for. This will vary from person to
person, from situation to situation and from time to time, but not
all that much. For most people most of the time we can be fairly
sure what things will be positively reinforcing. Giving people
things to eat and drink or things to wear are reinforcing. We
respond to such items naturally because they are, in the last resort,
necessary for life. Likewise, adults and most children respond to
attention and to social signals like gestures and statements of
approval. Such social signals, except perhaps smiling, which is a
very powerful one, have had to be learned. Such social gestures
become reinforcing through being associated with other reinforcers, like the natural ones mentioned above, on many occasions
from early on in life.

Some reinforcers, of which money is the best example, owe their reinforcing power to the fact that they give free access to other things which are in themselves reinforcing. Such reinforcers are called tokens and their great advantage is that they make it possible to reinforce immediately and in situations where the use of primary reinforcement would be difficult. This situation frequently obtains in schools and hence marks, stars and points are often used as tokens. It is important to realise that they are only effective when their power is understood and valued by all those involved. To begin with, therefore, they must be clearly linked with established reinforcers such as preferred activities or special treats of some sort or other.

In order to use reinforcement effectively we have to identify what is positively reinforcing for the pupil(s) in a given situation and then learn to use this knowledge to shape up desired behaviours whether social or academic. As stated above, we can only find out what is reinforcing to an individual, a group or a class by trying it out to see if it works but we can get some good ideas as to what is likely to be reinforcing by:

1.   observing pupils when they have freedom of choice, or

2.   by asking them what they like to do best.

Anything or any activity which a pupil enjoys and over which we have some control in school can be used as a reinforcer. Extra time to carry on some activity, to listen to records, to play games, to go out to break early, to help in the classroom, to use certain pieces of apparatus or just to be given a free choice of occupation have all been used successfully as positive reinforcers with children. Many of these activities can be educational in themselves. If we can make their availability dependent upon some clear criteria for behaviour over a certain period or in a certain situation then we shall begin to exert influence over that behaviour. For example, a few minutes extra on a favoured activity in P.E. can be made dependent upon an agreed level of quietness and/or speed in getting changed.

What do children regard as effective rewards and punishments?

A reservation which some primary teachers may have, initially, about Positive Teaching is that it can be difficult to determine effective rewards with troublesome or poorly motivated, older pupils. The disenchanted, potentially troublesome, child is less likely to find the privilege of feeding the guinea pig rewarding. So it is reasonable to ask, "What do primary aged pupils find rewarding?" To this end, we have carried out consumer surveys on this topic. A simple questionnaire was designed in which pupils were asked to select their answers to a series of questions from a number of alternatives. Despite the fact that the language was purposely kept very simple, each item and the list of answers was read aloud as pupils worked through the sheet. This was done because it was known that some children would have difficulty in reading the text with meaning and to ensure that no invidious distinctions should be made.

These surveys have, so far, been carried out only with secondary aged pupils. We plan to survey the views of primary school children in the near future. Nevertheless, we can speculate about the probable views of older junior school children on the basis of our findings from first year secondary pupils aged 11 to 12 years since their views are likely to be based, at least in part, on their recent primary school experiences. Our first secondary study included 80 first-year pupils attending two comprehensive schools in the West Midlands. The Praise and Rewards Attitude Questionnaire was employed to enquire into pupils' preferences for various types of reward for both academic work and classroom behaviour. It was found that most of the first-year pupils who took part perceived rewards and praise as appropriate outcomes for both. The results also showed that when offered a choice of six alternative rewards (sweets, free time, no reward, praise, points or a positive letter home), free time and a positive letter home were the most highly regarded. These younger pupils also valued sweets and points as rewards, which found less favour with the older ones. Free time was, perhaps, to be expected as an acceptable reward. It is relatively easy to arrange and has often been shown to be effective. A positive letter home was much less predictable and is hardly ever employed in primary schools. A letter home is normally used to convey disapproval of some aspect of social or academic behaviour.

A subsequent study replicated and extended these findings by using a very similar instrument to ask, in addition, what punishments and sanctions pupils considered to be effective in bringing about behaviour change. This survey included 183 first-year pupils, 96 boys and 87 girls. Once again, free time and a letter home were regarded as effective rewards for both academic work and classroom behaviour whilst the most effective punishments were perceived to be a letter home complaining about some aspect of work or behaviour and being put on report. These younger pupils, unlike their elders, regarded detention as an effective punishment. The least effective punishments, according to these pupils, were being sent out and being told off. The pupils involved were also asked about their views on the opinions of their teachers and of their peers about matters of discipline and work. Perhaps surprisingly, the vast majority (well over 90% of first-year pupils) claimed to value their teachers' opinions about their work and their conduct more highly than that of their peers.

If these findings are true of primary aged children as well then there appears to be a mis-match between the punishments and sanctions most used by teachers (like telling off and sending out) and those regarded as effective by their pupils. On the other hand some actions (both punishments and rewards) which are regarded as effective by pupils are seldom, if ever, used by teachers. An example of this is the positive letter home which, when used, has been found to be very effective. It would appear that further research is needed in this area if teachers' actions are to be more effective. In addition to teachers' and pupils' opinions we need to know much more about the incidence of praise and rewarding strategies, about how effective each is found to be and with which groups they will work and what efforts have been made to improve their effectiveness. Common sense would suggest that most of the punishments which uphold the rule systems of schools fall upon the very few, and have little effect.

Making reprimands more effective

Some teachers use reprimands quite frequently but not very effectively. We can tell that this is so because they are using them all the time. If their reprimands were effective in punishing a behaviour, that behaviour would be choked off and the reprimands would decrease accordingly. For example, a teacher may observe that one child is disturbing others in the class by his behaviour. He is not getting on with his own work and instead is preventing others from making progress with theirs. The teacher is not quite sure what to do but decides that he or she has to intervene in some way. The teacher shouts across the room, "Charlie, stop messing about and get on with your work or I'll come over there and sort you out". Unless this does have the intended effect and thereby stops Charlie misbehaving it will probably mean that the next time the teacher observes the same sort of event he or she will either ignore it, in the hope that it will cease, or be forced into some more serious confrontation.

Positive teachers do not ignore situations like these nor does Positive Teaching imply that reprimands should never be used. Reprimands have a very real place in the repertoire of positive teachers but they will prove to be most effective when they are used *infrequently* in a climate that is predominantly positive. In order to make reprimands effective they should be delivered from close quarters, not shouted across the room for everyone to hear. Reducing the personal distance allows the teacher to speak in a quiet but firm tone to make it perfectly clear that he or she is displeased with the behaviour that has been observed and does not intend that it shall continue. It is best if teachers can, at the same time, remain quite calm and show that they do not feel threatened by the situation. It may, occasionally, be necessary to spell out some consequence or sanction which will follow if the unwanted behaviour does not cease and this, too, is in keeping with the positive approach. Of course, the promised punishment or sanction must be reasonable and in accord with the common policy of the school and it must be carried out exactly as promised or the teacher's credibility and status will suffer. It is worth repeating, however, that reprimands are most effective when they are quiet and private and when used sparingly in a generally positive teaching context.

This is clearly illustrated in the following research study carried out in two third- and fourth-year junior classes. In both classes levels of on-task behaviour were low and both (female) teachers used quite a high rate of loud negative comments. The third-year class comprised 17 boys and eight girls whereas the fourth-year class was larger with 20 boys and 11 girls.

Both classes were initially observed for a series of half-hour sessions using the OPTIC schedule. After six observation sessions the teacher of the third-year class was asked to reduce her use of negative responses and to make them private. She was subsequently asked to increase her use of positive responses, again giving as many as possible privately. Similarly, the other teacher was asked to reduce her negatives and to make them private after 11 preliminary sessions and again, subsequently to increase her use of private praise statements. Both teachers successfully reduced their use of loud negatives but were less successful in increasing their use of private praise.

In the third-year class on-task behaviour rose from a low average of 35% to around 57% when reprimands were reduced and made more private. When increased private praise was added on-task behaviour improved only marginally more to 59%, on average. In the fourth-year class the average level of on-task behaviour rose from 59% to 68% when reprimands were reduced and made private and to 72% when private praise was included. These results show that teachers can use reprimands more sparingly and sensitively and to good effect. Some teachers, however, find it more difficult to increase their rates of praise.

These simple experimental interventions demonstrate first that teachers can change their behaviour by altering the way in which they respond to their pupils. Under guidance they can learn to become less negative and, within this context, to exercise more effective control of misbehaviour. Secondly, the experiments showed that when teachers changed their behaviour, pupils' behaviour changed too. This resulted in classroom conditions which were more agreeable to both teachers and children and which were likely to be more conducive to good academic outcomes.

We can keep our use of reprimands to a low level by employing alternative, more positive strategies. Positive teachers seek to avoid conflict wherever possible. Instead of using reprimands teachers can simply ignore some trivial incidents completely. The use of reprimands often proves to be counter-productive since we know that the inappropriate behaviour of some children is reinforced by the attention they get from teacher reprimands (so-called attention seeking behaviour). If teachers continually comment adversely on every minor misdemeanour they can sometimes make matters worse.

We recently carried out an intriguing small-scale study with one of our students which demonstrates the importance of teacher praise and approval. Two female teachers were observed with their classes of 11 year-olds. The first class comprised 16 boys and 14 girls and the second had 16 boys and 15 girls. Following preliminary observations in both classes the teachers were asked to change their teaching styles.

In the first class on-task behaviour averaged 83%. The teacher was then asked to reduce her praise to the absolute minimum and she succeeded in eliminating almost all praise statements. As a result on-task behaviour dropped to 76% and rose again to 81% when normal conditions were resumed. We then asked her to eliminate praise and increase her use of reprimands and this time on-task behaviour fell to 74%. Finally, when normal conditions were resumed on-task behaviour rose again back to 83%. In the second class on-task behaviour averaged 87% during preliminary observations falling marginally to 84% when the teacher was asked to eliminate her use of praise. It rose again to 89% when normal conditions were resumed.

This is a telling study made possible only by the willingness of teachers to collaborate with our rather bizarre requests. Although only small-scale it confirms some early American research which demonstrated how good classes could be made more disruptive by reducing praise and increasing reprimands. The message is clear. Keep your praise rates high and minimise the use of reprimands (ignoring altogether some trivial misbehaviours) if you want to enjoy good classroom discipline. Before leaving this topic, however, we would not want to give the impression that ignoring, used on its own, is some sort of panacea. We are concerned that some educational psychologists have, in the past, over-emphasised the importance of ignoring and have not stressed sufficiently that it will only be effective when used in conjunction with other, more positive procedures. We will return to this point again in Chapter Five when we discuss the powerful behaviour management strategy known as *rules, praise and ignoring*.

Another alternative to reprimanding a pupil for misbehaving is to ask him or her, in a neutral tone of voice, what he or she should be doing. This serves two purposes. First, the articulation of the nature of the task by the pupil may prompt the appropriate behaviour. Secondly, this may reveal a genuine misunderstanding that the pupil is experiencing about the nature of the work. Clearly, if they do not know exactly what they have to do pupils are more likely to misbehave. Many good teachers have other, more positive ways of dealing with misbehaviour than using reprimands. Some use humour to good effect to defuse the situation. It must be emphasised, however, that we do mean humour, not sarcasm which, in any case, young children may not understand. Finally, we should remember that we all like, and deserve, to be treated with respect. The abrupt manner of speaking, sometimes verging on rudeness, that some teachers employ, can be quite offensive to other adults and very hurtful to children.

A point which we have already made and which summarises all of our suggested strategies for dealing with misbehaviour is "Act, don't react". By this we mean that teachers should think carefully and in advance about how they are going to respond to troublesome behaviour. Rather than reacting emotionally without thinking, teachers should try to respond in a considered manner worthy of a professional.

Improving your positives

As we have already intimated, it follows logically that if you can increase the amount of time that pupils spend behaving appropriately there is less time for them to behave inappropriately. By accentuating the positive we can reduce the necessity for negatives. In this section we will consider how we can improve our use of praise so as to make it more effective.

Praise is most effective when it is sincere and natural. Some people seem to use more praise than others but we all use praise sometimes and we can all improve our rate of praising. As we have said before, we should aim to use a variety of praise statements and make use of appropriate gestures and actions to accompany them. Similarly, we need to be sensitive in our use of praise and to be sure that praise is given only contingently.

One of the most powerful groups of reinforcers is the social response of adults, like attention and praise, physical closeness and facial expressions, like smiling. Note that here we are not referring to general pleasantness or otherwise of teachers' attitudes and contacts with children but the specific use of social reinforcers to bring about change in behaviour. What matters is *when* the teacher praises *whom*, and for *what* behaviour.

As suggested earlier, some people are very good at making these social responses towards others and we all use them sometimes, but we can all learn to use them more effectively. Most teachers seem to believe that they are already very positive in their responses to their pupils but, as we have shown in Chapter Two, this is not true of all. We have to remember also that many of our younger pupils have not yet learned to recognise and respond to the rather subtle social signals that adults use to communicate their feelings about each other. This is not a cause for despair but rather a challenge to our skills in teaching. We may have to teach children how to engage the attention of adults, how to address them, how to express an alternative point of view without giving offence, how to break off an exchange politely and so on. This too can, and should, be done positively, not by nagging and chiding, and may be considered as an appropriate part of our broader curricular remit.

When using praise and rewards we need to consider what can be said, how it can be said and what we can use as a source of positive reinforcement. How we say these things or carry out these actions is almost as important as what we say or do. If you are not sure how enthusiastic you look when doing or saying these things try using a mirror; in private, of course! There is no doubt that practice will improve one's ability to dispense positive social reinforcement effectively and it costs nothing.

Casual observations of teachers working with young children in nursery and infant classes reveals that touch is frequently and freely employed. Our research has shown, however, that teachers rarely use touch to accompany praise.

We carried out two studies to examine the effectiveness of teacher touch to accompany praise for young children's classroom behaviour. Our first study was carried out in two infant classes taught by experienced, female teachers. Each teacher and her class were first observed for ten half-hour sessions using a version of the OPTIC schedule to determine the amount of time they spent getting on with their work. Following these ten sessions, both teachers were asked to touch children only when they praised them for appropriate work or behaviour and to try not to touch children for other purposes. It was emphasised that no deliberate increase of praise was required or to be attempted. Both teachers were again observed, as before, for a further ten sessions. Both teachers successfully increased their use of touch to accompany praise and decreased their use of other touch. In both classes, when teachers touched children together with praising them, the amount of time children spent getting on with their work rose by over 15%, from around 75% to 90%, and disruptive behaviour fell from about ten or eleven instances per session to only two or three.

The second study was carried out with two further infant classes. The touch procedure was introduced into the second class a week after being introduced into the first class. Again, both classes were taught by experienced, female teachers. Each teacher and her class were observed, as before, for three weeks. The teacher of the first class was instructed to alter her use of touch after one week whereas in the other class, two weeks elapsed before the teacher was asked to change her use of touch. We then observed for a further two weeks in the first class and a further one week in the second.

Again, both teachers were successful in reducing their use of "other" touch and in increasing their use of touch accompanying praise. As a result, for the first class, the amount of time children spent getting on with their work increased from about 40% to nearly 70% and for the other class from 50% to 65%.

These two studies taken together, involving four teachers, provide convincing evidence for the effectiveness of using teacher touch to accompany praise when teaching classes of young children. In all four classes, the amount of time children spent working increased substantially, by an average of 20%. In other words, over the four classes, children spent about a third as much time again working compared with previous levels.

By using positive touch in association with praise, teachers will be helping young children to experience the rewarding effects of teacher praise. Verbal praise may not be very meaningful to some young children, especially those from home backgrounds where the first language is not English, but accompanied by positive teacher touch, its meaning is clear. In early childhood education, this "touching way to teach" may prove highly effective and rewarding for both teachers and children.

Generally speaking it has been found that statements of both praise and blame are most effective in bringing about change in pupils' behaviour when they take the form of what we call REX responses. Such responses can be regarded as belonging to one of three categories although the distinction between them is not really of great importance. If the classroom is one where rules have been agreed and are clearly manifest it is possible for the teacher to refer to the fact that a pupil has succeeded in carrying out an agreed rule. The teacher can say, "Thanks Susan, you've remembered our rule about putting up your hand". This would be an example of an R response where the teacher had related praise to the keeping of an agreed rule. Sometimes teachers couple praise with drawing attention to a pupil's work or behaviour in terms of setting a good example. Such E responses are quite useful when the teacher wants to draw attention to the fact that a certain student has performed well or produced a good example of the work set. Most primary teachers use display areas in order to exhibit work they feel is of special worth. At other times they may send the pupil to a senior member of staff to show what has been achieved or an improvement that has been made.

The third category of REX responses (X responses) comprises cases where teachers spell out precisely (eXactly) what it is that they are pleased about. In a sense the two preceding cases do just this, but in a particular way. By using X responses teachers make it absolutely clear to pupils what they are pleased about. Some teachers give quite a high level of positive responses in terms of saying "Good" or "Well done", but the pupils are sometimes not quite sure what they have been praised for. Is it the appearance of the work, the quantity that has been produced or the fact that most of it has been completed correctly? It is very important that children should know exactly what they are being praised or blamed for.

It is worth repeating our earlier point that verbal comment, whether of praise or blame, should be directed at the act performed, rather than at the person who has performed it. There is a great deal of difference between commenting on a good or bad act and saying that you are a bad or good person. To imply that a pupil is a bad person lays us open to the charge of labelling. We know well enough that once a pupil acquires a reputation for being bad it tends to become a self-fulfilling prophecy. Teachers begin to expect such children to behave badly and to look for corroborating evidence for their expectations whilst the individuals themselves begin to regard themselves as marked out for special attention. Both eventualities are to be avoided. Likewise, it does a pupil no good to be regarded as special because of a reputation for good work or behaviour. It can place unwarranted strain on a child from both staff and fellow students.

It is important for teachers to be aware of how much positive reinforcement they are using and how many negative consequences they are providing. One way of doing this is to use a hand tally-counter to record positive and negative responses as described in Chapter Two. Of course, if you are counting negatives the fact that you are holding the tally-counter in your hand is bound to inhibit your giving of negative responses to your pupils. Just as you are about to shout at someone for inappropriate behaviour you will be aware of the tally-counter and will refrain. The result will not be a very accurate count of your usual number of negative responses but this does not matter if your intention is to reduce them. On the other hand, if you are counting your positive responses with a view to increasing their number, the tally-counter will again be a cue for you to be positive because every time you are positive you will be able to notch up one more tally. It will encourage you to look for appropriate behaviour and to reinforce it.

We routinely ask our students to carry out exercises in which they record their use of positives and negatives. For example, one of our student teachers decided to monitor her own performance on teaching practice using a tally-counter. During the first week she made no effort to change her behaviour and recorded, on average, 6 positives and 16 negatives during her 15-minute self-observation periods. She then attempted to change her own behaviour over the following four weeks and with great success. She managed to increase her positives to just over 13 and her use of negatives dropped to around 4, per session, on average. To put it another way, she changed from using nearly three times as many negatives as positives to using more than three times as many positives as negatives. If a young student teacher can achieve results like these when under the stress of teaching practice, it should be possible for experienced teachers to do at least as well. We appreciate, of course, that experienced teachers may well have some unlearning to do.

Using a tally-counter certainly makes you more aware of the nature of your responses but if you really want to know how many positive and negative responses you give in a typical lesson, and this is interesting information for any teacher, then you really need to have somebody else to do the observing for you. Perhaps you can find a colleague who will watch you for a period and give you some objective feedback (using a tally-counter, maybe) and then you can change places on another occasion. In addition, it would be salutary for all of us to have someone count how many opportunities we miss of applying a positive response appropriately to good work or behaviour and how often we give a reward when little has been done to deserve it. The same can apply in the opposite direction to the negative consequences we employ. Another way of getting some more objective feedback rather than using the tally-counter yourself is to make a tape-recording of your lesson and then listen to it later on. Of course, this will only pick up what you say but these statements will probably include most of the responses you make to your pupils.

What appears to be critical about the response rates of teachers is the ratio between positive and negative responses. Clearly there will be certain optimum rates of responding. On the one hand some teachers are very non-responsive whilst some submit their pupils to a barrage of comment and feedback. The appropriate level of comment from teachers will vary from situation to situation and from teacher to teacher but it would appear that where good teaching and learning is taking place positive comment usually far outweighs the negative. In cases where the balance has been predominantly negative and where teachers have managed to change this, a change in the level of pupil on-task behaviour has been observed to follow. For example, one of our students, an experienced teacher, carried out a useful study with a student teacher on final teaching practice. Preliminary observations revealed that the student teacher was using almost three times as many negative as positive responses. She was then instructed in the basic principles of Positive Teaching and decided that she would attempt to provide more positive responses to her pupils and to reduce her use of negatives. Subsequent observations showed that she was able to change her behaviour markedly, now giving eight times as many positive as negative responses. As a result pupil on-task behaviour increased from around 55% to nearly 75%. When she was observed again a few weeks later on-task behaviour was still over 70%.

Many of our students have carried out studies demonstrating the power of praise when given systematically and contingently by teachers. The following four studies are typical examples. The first was in a class of children aged between 4 and 5 in a reception class. Their teacher was a woman with five years experience of teaching. She was accustomed to using quite a lot of praise but it tended to be rather vague and non-specific. The aim of the study was to encourage her to use more REX responses to the behaviour of her children, i.e. to make it clear to them what she was praising them for.

The teacher and her class were observed on four occasions in each of the three phases of the study using the OPTIC schedule. In the first phase of preliminary observations before the intervention began, the teacher was giving about 48 positive statements every lesson but only ten of these, on average, was specific. The on-task level of the children in the class averaged 59%. Once she began to try to be more specific she was able to increase her praise statements to 62, on average, and 40 of these were now REX responses. The immediate result was that the on-task behaviour of the children in her class rose to 79%. In the third phase she was asked to stop trying to use REX responses. The number of praise statements fell to 45 of which only 9 were REX responses, whilst the on-task level for the class fell back to 65%.

The second study took place in a class of 34 top juniors, 10-11 year-olds whose rather inexperienced teacher rarely gave praise or approval to their work or behaviour. The level of teacher praise was monitored and the behaviour of one group of four girls and four boys was observed. The teacher did not know which children were being observed. In order to carry out this study two observers were employed, one to watch the teacher and one to observe the children. In each phase of the study there were four observation sessions.

Preliminary observations indicated that the teacher was giving only six positives on average per lesson and that the on-task level of the children was 71%. Once the intervention began the teacher managed to raise her positive responses to an average of 23 per lesson and the on-task level rose to 90%. In the last phase when she allowed her rate of positive responding to fall again to about 11 per lesson the on-task level of the children fell to 76%.

The third study was carried out with another woman teacher with eight years of teaching experience. Her class comprised 17 boys and nine girls aged between 9 and 10. Observation of the class indicated that the boys were much more involved in verbal interactions in the classroom than the girls even when the disparity in numbers was taken into account. The purpose of the study was to see whether the teacher could increase the relative number of verbal contributions made by the girls in this class by the judicious use of praise.

Preliminary observations over a period of two weeks showed that the average number of verbal responses made by the children, per hour, was 152. An adjustment to figures was made to take account of the imbalance in numbers between boys and girls and this showed that boys contributed 107 to this total and the girls only 45. During the operational part of this study the teacher was asked to increase her rate of praise for children's verbal responses and especially to those of the girls by moving closer to them when responding and to be fulsome in her praise. Typically, she would say something like, "That was an excellent answer, Well done!" or "It's really nice to have our girls joining in so well". The result was that the total number of verbal responses by children rose to 240, an increase of 58%. The proportional contribution of the boys after an allowance had been made for the different numbers involved was 116, an increase of 8%. The girls, on the other hand, were observed to have increased their proportional contribution to 123, an increase of 173%. This was achieved simply by the differential use of teacher praise in response to the children's verbal contributions to her lessons.

The fourth study involved a class of 34 top juniors and their young, female and relatively inexperienced teacher who claimed that she did not "find it necessary to give praise". (This reminds us of the teacher who wrote to a colleague: "Having tried everything else with this child, I have now resorted to praising her"!) She was observed, using OPTIC, for four preliminary sessions and the on-task behaviour of a group of eight children in her class was monitored. Following these sessions she was asked to praise the pupils in her class in an active positive way when they were on-task. To help her in this she was told that one of the groups of children (she did not know which) would record the number of praise statements they received. She was also made aware of the importance of contingency and consistency in giving out praise and four more sessions were observed. This was then discontinued and a week later a further four sessions were observed when she was teaching normally. The intervention was successful in increasing her praise rate to nearly four times what it had been during the preliminary observations but it fell back to about twice the original rate during the final observations. The average on-task level of the selected group of children rose from 72% to 90% when praise was introduced and fell back to around 77% during the last four observations. This study clearly demonstrates the powerful effect of simply increasing contingent praise.

These small-scale studies show that simple praise strategies work well with primary aged children. Note also that the improvement in behaviour occurred with each class only when the teacher improved her use of praise and that it deteriorated again when she stopped.

Supplementing praise with other strategies

The effective use of praise and encouragement will probably be sufficient to bring about a co-operative atmosphere conducive to learning for many classes for most of the time. Occasionally, however, we encounter pupils or even whole classes which do not respond so readily. Alternatively, even with well-motivated pupils and classes, there will be times when the teacher may wish to encourage even greater effort or to teach other, more mature social behaviours. In these cases we may wish to supplement praise with other strategies including, perhaps, the use of other rewards.

Some visual record of progress is a good provider of reinforcement. This is the function of wall-charts showing tokens of achievement but inter-pupil rivalry is not generally part of Positive Teaching. Teachers already use tokens of some sort (points or stars on a star chart, perhaps) in order to motivate their pupils and allow competition between groups in order to stimulate improvement. For example, an arrangement may be made by which the winning of points or tokens depends upon improvement in work or behaviour. However, teachers frequently arrange matters so that the reward goes to the group which gets most points. This is fine so long as the competition is close, but once the members of one group observe that they are far behind the rest with no chance of catching up, all the motivational effect for them disappears. If there is to be an element of winning, it must be open to all, equally. Rather than promising a reward of some sort to the team or individual getting the best score it is better to set a reasonable target such that all who reach that criterion may have access to the rewarding consequences. By this means everyone is in the race until the end and, as in the caucus race in *Alice in Wonderland*, it is possible for everyone to be a winner so long as they make an effort to improve.

From the surveys, reported earlier, we should remember that free time was highly valued by 11 to 12 year-olds and that a positive letter home was the next most highly valued. These younger pupils also valued house points as rewards. These and other rewards such as the opportunity to choose an activity, listen to music or to use special apparatus can all be used to supplement praise. But a little imagination and discussion with pupils will generate a host of other rewarding activities and special treats which can be given on an occasional basis to a class which continues to work well. We have heard of positive teachers who organise baked bean toasted sandwich parties and video sessions at half-term for classes which work well. This may not be your style but you can probably come up with equally appealing alternatives.

The best competition for a pupil is with him or herself in comparison with earlier performance. Some older primary pupils will be well able to record their own progress in academic output or in social behaviour if they are shown how and they are usually very willing and interested to do it. A truly objective record of their own performance would give them a much more realistic base from which to judge their own progress. We will return to this important issue of self-recording in Chapter Five where we will also discuss other effective classroom strategies for teaching and maintaining high levels of appropriate classroom behaviour.

Further reading

Further details of our work on pupil preferences for varying forms of reward and punishment are reported in the following article:

Houghton, S., Merrett, F. and Wheldall, K. (1988). The attitudes of British secondary school pupils to praise, rewards, punishment and reprimands. *New Zealand Journal of Educational Studies, 23,* 203-214.

Our study describing teachers' use of touch in infants schools may be found in:

Wheldall, K., Bevan, K. and Shortall, K. (1986). A touch of reinforcement: the effects of contingent teacher touch on the classroom behaviour of young children. *Educational Review, 38,* 207-216.

Numerous examples of simple studies involving increased praise are reported in:

Merrett, F. (1986). *Encouragement Works Better Than Punishment* (second edition). Birmingham: Positive Products.

Wheldall, K. and Merrett, F. (1984). *Positive Teaching: the behavioural approach.* London: Allen & Unwin, reprinted 1989 by Positive Products, Birmingham.

Chapter Five
DEVELOPING EFFECTIVE CLASSROOM STRATEGIES

Good classroom behaviour will not necessarily ensure effective academic learning but it is, in our view, an essential prerequisite. Clearly, pupils will find it more difficult to work in a noisy and disruptive environment. Positive Teaching, as we have tried to make clear throughout this book, is concerned with identifying and increasing appropriate behaviour in the classroom. Positive Teaching is not about being repressive in order to reduce unacceptable behaviour. We reject the notion of the teacher as a form of Dalek continually on the look-out for misbehaviour in order to exterminate it. In this chapter we will be discussing how teachers can develop effective classroom strategies for encouraging appropriate behaviour.

Before we progress to this, however, let us consider certain key issues which underpin the whole enterprise. If we are attempting to teach certain new forms of behaviour or to increase the rate of behaviours which already occur but only infrequently, then there are several important ground rules which must be applied. Whatever is chosen as a reinforcer must be applied:

1. Contingently. It must be arranged so that the reinforcer follows the behaviour every time it occurs but is not available otherwise. For example, an infants teacher might make sure that a star is given every time a child puts up his or her hand to ask a question, but not otherwise.

2. Immediately. There must be no waiting between the act and the reinforcer as there would be in the situation where the teacher tries to motivate the student by saying, "If you work hard for the whole term you will get a good report". Consider here what is meant by work hard in terms of pin-pointing behaviour. So many of the rewards which are offered by education and in

schools generally are of this long-term nature and do not constitute proper rewards at all in the context of Positive Teaching. Think of some of the children you teach and consider how the school is rewarding them day by day for efforts that they may be making to improve their work or behaviour. Your most probable conclusion will be "not a lot". Praise and rewards can both be given immediately.

3. Consistently. This is one of the chief elements in Positive Teaching. If children find that they are allowed to behave in a certain way on one day whilst on the next they are punished for the same behaviour, they are being deprived of the opportunity of finding out how the rule system works. A pupil can learn the rules which operate in a particular situation only if the consequences can be relied upon. Many children who have difficulty in behaving appropriately in the classroom have come from previous regimes (the home, for example) which lacked such consistency, so that to provide a consistent regime for all pupils should be one of the chief aims of positive teachers.

4. Abundantly. The first few steps made by the child which are recognised to be in the right direction must be given abundant reward. This is probably not going to be easy because pupils who do not perform very well or whose behaviour is rather poor are not going to make sudden and large-scale improvements at first. The improvements that such pupils are likely to make will be very small; hardly discernible, perhaps, unless the teacher is a very good and practised observer. This is why Positive Teaching places such stress on the importance of careful pin-pointing, counting and recording of behaviour. To begin with, every instance of appropriate behaviour should be rewarded at once because this has been found to be the most effective way to bring about change in behaviour.

Once the desired behaviour has been learned and is occurring frequently enough the task of the positive teacher has changed. He or she now has the job of maintaining the newly learned behaviour and for that different procedures are needed. It has been found that the best way of maintaining behaviour once it has been learned is to provide intermittent reinforcement as a consequence rather than the continuous and abundant reinforcement necessary to teach it in the first place. This is done by arranging for reinforcement to occur less frequently and less immediately. In other words, we allow a leaner rate of reinforcement to be adopted so that in time two or three good responses may be required to obtain a reward and, by degrees, the child is made to wait longer for the reward to come. This process of gradually reducing the relative level of rewarding by small amounts (known as fading) should then continue until the behaviours are maintained by the infrequent rewards which occur naturally and which serve to maintain most human social conduct.

It must be stressed that it is very important that these changes in the rewarding process should be made very gradually. They should not be started until the new behaviour has been thoroughly learned and care must be taken to see that there is no falling off while the fading process is under way. If fading begins too soon or happens too quickly then ground won will soon be lost. We can see how behaviour is maintained by natural consequences by use of a simple example. It is only occasionally that people respond to our courteous waiting for them to pass through a doorway first but it does happen sometimes and that is enough to maintain our behaviour. It is worth mentioning at this stage that teachers are not into the business of making saints. We do not expect perfect behaviour from our pupils but rather a standard that is reasonable both for them and for others. Of paramount importance in all our dealings with children are the principles of justice and consistency. Nothing upsets them more than to realise that they are being treated unfairly. Rules of conduct apply to all, to us as well as the children we teach.

A common reaction to Positive Teaching, however, is that such an approach would only work with very young children. Many teachers are sceptical of success with classes of older children, believing that at best it would necessitate highly complex and time-consuming procedures. In fact, we have now carried out a number of studies which demonstrate the effectiveness of simple strategies even with classes of *secondary* school children.

The methods we advocate are all firmly based on the principles of Positive Teaching and have all been carefully and rigorously tried and tested in work with teachers. Simple and straightforward interventions by teachers using positive methods can bring about dramatic results in terms of improved classroom atmosphere and the quantity and quality of work produced. Both antecedents and consequences can be used to good effect to change behaviour. Moreover, these methods , illustrated in the case studies below, have been shown to yield more satisfying and rewarding classroom experiences for both teachers and children.

Positive Teaching can be applied in the management of classroom social behaviour in an endless variety of ways, calling for imagination, inventiveness and initiative on the part of teachers. There is no single prescriptive nostrum. Positive Teaching requires the consistent application of basic principles to unique and personal classroom problems as the following examples will illustrate.

The teacher of a reception class found that when the children, aged 4 to 5 years old, were playing with toys like Lego or stickle-bricks or when using apparatus like Unifix, beads for threading or shapes for sorting, the floor became littered with dropped pieces. Accordingly, a great deal of time was wasted clearing up at the end of the session. She felt that apart from the time-wasting there was another issue, namely, the need to teach children to be aware of objects that had been dropped and the necessity of retrieving them, there and then, before they were damaged or lost.

The teacher had two groups of between 18 and 20 children coming to her at separate times for certain sessions. These she designated red and green groups. She explained to the children that at the end of each five minutes of the twenty minute session a timer would sound. (A kitchen timer was used for this purpose.) If the floor, at that time, was clear of pieces the group would receive a green (or red) star to be stuck on a chart which was prominently displayed on the wall. Each group could thus earn four stars in a session.

The effects were immediate. On most occasions when the timer sounded the teacher looked at the floor and found it to be clear.

After five sessions the stars were totalled and it was found that the red group had 13 stars and the green group 14. Each child was given a Smartie for trying whilst the members of the green group had an additional Smartie for having most stars.

The result was time saved in clearing up, a successful attempt to keep the floor tidy and a lesson in awareness and responsibility. This intervention was soundly based from the behavioural point of view since the task was clearly within the competence of these young children whilst the reward system allowed for no losers: a very important point, especially with such young children. The stars were easy for the teacher to handle and were displayed on a chart that was clearly visible so that the children could see what progress they were making. Note that the task objectives were made realistic in that quite short periods of time were involved since children would find it easier to cope.

Next we describe two studies carried out by the teacher of a group of 29 seven to eight year-olds in a junior school. The teacher felt that the children were not concentrating sufficiently on their work. They spent a lot of their time chatting, playing around and generally distracting those seated nearby. An attempt was made to increase on-task behaviour and, hence, the output of work.

The procedure was explained to the children just as they were about to begin working individually at a set exercise. During the lesson the teacher moved around the classroom correcting work and so on. As she did so she was observing the children carefully and any child seen to be getting on particularly well or doing good work was praised and allowed to go to the front of the class in order to place a coloured bead in a dish placed there for the purpose. If the teacher observed a child who was not getting on, he or she was required to place a black bead in another, separate dish. The game was generally played for about 30 minutes at a time when a balance would be struck between the contents of the two dishes to see whether their good behaviours outweighed the less good.

In her other intervention the same teacher used groups into which the children were already organised for working as the basis for a game. The teacher would be sitting in front of the class and hearing children read to her. The children were told that she would be looking from time to time to observe the groups and that she would tally her record if all the members of the group were working. Times for looking up and the order for the groups to be looked at were not controlled. The teacher reports that before the study she looked up more often than not to tell a child to stop talking or to get on with his or her work, to sit down or something similar. When this game was in operation she looked up and commented only when a group had succeeded in doing something that she had asked them to do.

In both cases the result was an increase in the incidence of on-task behaviour and an improvement in the amount of written work produced when compared with that achieved in similar sessions before the experiments. The teacher reported that many of the children surprised themselves by the amount of work they pro- duced; instead of a few lines they now managed to complete the whole of the set exercise in the given time. She also felt that the giving of praise improved the children's confidence and thus caused them to try harder the next time. However, the teacher found that having the children come to the front of the class in the first game to place their beads tended to be disruptive, so at a later stage she placed the beads in the dishes herself and this proved to be a great improvement. To be truly positive she ought to have dropped the idea of using black beads for inappropriate behaviour.

Both these interventions are examples of consciously applied strategies which cause the teacher to pay attention to good behav- iour and (largely) to ignore unwanted acts. The results are just what positive teachers would expect. Both these games would have been improved if some more objective definition of working and good behaviour had been given. This is where some positive rules (as discussed in Chapter Four) would have been useful so that the positive reinforcement given could then have been related to specific rules, as we shall see.

The next study was carried out by the teacher of a group of 33 children of mixed ability aged 9 to 10. The problem was that they made a lot of noise when moving about the school. This included coming in from the playground at the beginning of sessions and moving from the classroom to the hall and back for P.E. The teacher believed that part of the problem lay in the antecedent conditions. When coming in from the playground the children were required to make two lines, one for boys and one for girls. This meant that two very long lines were formed in which the children tended to jostle each other to be first or last. The corridor from the playground to the classroom was very long, as was that from the classroom to the hall. In addition, there were two corners to be negotiated and a set of fire doors. This meant that it was impossible for the teacher to keep an eye on all the children as they moved about the school. If the teacher stayed behind, the children in front would race ahead whilst if she led the file, children at the back lagged behind and became noisy. Most of the other classes in the school behaved in much the same way but, being smaller, did not appear to create so much confusion.

School policy required that children should learn to go about the school quietly but the teacher had enjoyed no success in changing the behaviour pattern by using traditional means, i.e. shouting at the children or making them all come back to carry out the manoeuvre again. She decided, therefore, to change the antecedent conditions. The children were given instructions to form three lines in future. There were thus only eleven children in each line and they were given set positions so that there would be no pushing for places in future. Particularly noisy children were separated from each other, three being appointed to act as line leaders. The leaders were given strategic stopping places, for example at the corners, so that the teacher could control the movement more easily. After reorganisation of the lines the whole exercise was made into a game, to show that this was the best class in the school. The class were reading a book called *A Dog and a Half* at this time and the teacher suggested that the class should call itself "A Class and a Half". From this point on the teacher indicated approval by using social reinforcement in terms of encouraging words and gestures as each stopping point was reached without noise or fuss. This change in behaviour was noted by the class next door and the friendly rivalry which this engendered between the two groups was encouraged by both teachers.

This strategy proved to be extremely effective. Other teachers commented quite spontaneously on the "quiet class coming up the corridor" and when their previous teacher made such a comment it was particularly rewarding for the children. The giving of social reinforcement was continued for some time and every so often treats of one sort or another were contrived when the children did well. Gradually, the reinforcement was reduced to the occasional, "Well done" or a reminder just before the class left the room. Soon the class learned to move quietly and at a moderate pace about the school and classes other than the one next door began to follow suit.

We see here how the teacher used a change in the antecedent conditions together with social reinforcement very skilfully to bring about desired behaviour change. At the same time she managed to use competition in a way that caused no harm to any individual. Perhaps of even greater significance is the way she managed to achieve a high degree of generalisation so that the behaviour was being maintained by naturally occurring contingencies. This, after all, is the goal of all positive teachers.

Implementing rules, praise and ignoring

One of the most useful and widely used techniques in Positive Teaching is known as RPI or rules, praise and ignoring. In brief, it requires the teacher first to negotiate with pupils a set of three or four short, positively phrased rules covering acceptable classroom behaviour, as described in Chapter Three. These often take the form of simple declarations of intent such as, "We try to get on with our work quietly" or "We put up our hands when we want to ask a question". Thinking in terms of the ABC model we outlined earlier it will be appreciated that rules are being employed here as important antecedents for behaviour. They act as a form of prompt or cue for appropriate behaviour. Teachers operating RPI are encouraged to draw attention to the rules regularly, preferably when pupils are clearly keeping the rules, but *not* when they are being infringed.

Both praise and ignoring refer to the consequences aspect of this procedure. Quite simply, teachers are required to praise pupils for keeping the rules (to "catch them being good") and to ignore infractions. Praise may refer to the whole class or to individuals but should refer specifically to their behaviour in keeping the rules.

As we have said, ignoring is often more difficult for teachers and is frequently misunderstood. It refers only to the behaviours governed by the rules and does not mean that teachers should not intervene if a fight breaks out or if pupils are about to do something dangerous. The idea is to avoid responding to rule-related misbehaviours since to do so may be counter-productive if the pupils involved find any form of teacher attention rewarding. It also detracts from the overall positive approach.

It must be emphasised that ignoring on its own (without rules and praise) is unlikely to be effective and as a technique it has certainly been over-sold to teachers. "Ignore it and it will go away" is the sloppy advice sometimes given to teachers by advisers and educational psychologists. This is, of course, total nonsense to professionals who know that they cannot permit certain behaviour excesses to continue without intervention and who recognise that their attention to certain behaviours, such as those involved in showing off to peers, has little effect in comparison with peer approval or attention. An unsuccessful or unpopular child who gets a little begrudging acceptance or a laugh from his or her peers for fooling about is often not going to be much affected by teacher reprimand or by ignoring. The technique of ignoring is at least partly predicated upon the assumption that teacher attention (even if negative) may be rewarding. The hard truth is that teacher response may be irrelevant.

Over the years our students have completed numerous studies involving RPI procedures which testify to their effectiveness. Studies have been carried out with pupils of various ages and in different settings, as the following examples will demonstrate. In this first example, carried out in a nursery class, the female teacher was anxious to encourage more appropriate behaviour at break time when the children had their milk, a piece of fruit and, occasionally, other food items. Her aim was to reduce the time wasting caused by "messing about" which was cutting into the time available for language and number activities. Consequently, she opted for an approach based on RPI. The forty children were observed on five mornings using the OPTIC schedule to measure time on-task. On-task behaviours included drinking milk, eating the food provided, being in seat and talking quietly to a neighbour when they had finished. During the second week of the study three rules were formulated and these were: we sit quietly at milk time, we drink our milk through the straw and we talk quietly when we have finished. The children were reminded of the rules at the beginning of each milk time and the nursery staff were asked to praise children who were on-task, e.g. "Look at Sunil, he has nearly finished his milk already". During the preliminary observations children were on-task for 59% of the time and 71% of milk bottles were emptied. When RPI was introduced the average on-task level rose to 88% and 83% of bottles were emptied.

In the next study, six preliminary observations were made of a first-year junior class, using the OPTIC schedule. These observations revealed a very high average level of on-task behaviour at around 80%. A group of six children was identified, however, who appeared to be less attentive than the rest. A further four observations of this specific group showed that their average on-task level was only about 68%. Consequently a very simple form of RPI was established for the whole class in which only one rule was negotiated and implemented. This was "We get on with our work when asked". Infractions of the rule were ignored while those pupils keeping the rule were heartily praised. A treat, such as playing a favourite game with the teacher or hearing a short reading from a favourite book, was also arranged to supplement praise. The results were remarkable. Observations over the next four sessions showed on-task behaviour averaging 98%! A simple word count showed that the amount of written work completed rose from an average of 37 words per child before the RPI strategy to 58 afterwards. This is further proof that increased on-task behaviour is usually accompanied by increases in the amount of work produced.

Some teachers have chosen to develop their RPI interventions and convert the strategy into a sort of game which they play with the class. In this first example, one of our earliest studies, the subject was a young, relatively inexperienced, female teacher who was having a lot of trouble in controlling her class of 30 intellectually below average 10-11 year-olds. Classroom seating was arranged around four tables and we decided to make use of this in our intervention strategy.

Initially, we needed more specific and accurate information about the children's behaviour in the classroom. A cassette-tape was prepared to give a clear signal at irregular intervals but on average once per minute. On hearing the sound the teacher would look at one of the four tables of children, indicated in random order on a prepared sheet, and note the behaviour of the target child for that table by ticking the appropriate column. The target child was chosen afresh for each observation session on a random basis and thus all children in the class were observed during the study. Every time she heard the signal the teacher had to glance at the schedule to see which table was next and record the behaviour of the target child by ticking appropriately. She could do this whilst working at her desk and, with experience, whilst walking around the room advising individuals and commenting on their work.

Preliminary observations revealed that the children were on-task for about 44% of the time. The teacher was then given some basic instruction in Positive Teaching methods and she chose to implement a game strategy. Briefly, the children were told the rules of a game which were: we stay in our seats whilst working, we get on quietly with our work and we try not to interrupt. Whilst the game was in progress, the cassette would be switched on and every time the signal sounded the teacher would look at one of the tables. If everyone on the table was keeping the rules, then each child on the table would score a house point. (They were assured that all tables would get equal turns but that the order would be random.) Each time a team point was given it was accompanied by verbal praise.

This procedure lasted for five weeks when an amendment was announced. In future points would be awarded on only 50% of the signals, again on a random basis. The signals continued to serve the teacher as a cue for observing and recording the behaviour of the target children as well as a signal for reinforcing rule keeping.

The results were remarkable and immediate. Average on-task behaviour rose from 44% to 77% following the introduction of the game. Moreover, when the amendment was made, after five weeks, the on-task behaviour rose even higher to between 80% and 100%. The quality of off-task behaviour also changed. Whereas before the intervention disruptiveness was mainly shown in loud talking and quite a lot of movement around the room, after the intervention off-task behaviour consisted mainly of passive inattention, daydreaming, watching other children and so on.

An attempt was also made to measure academic output both before and after the intervention. For example, samples of written work taken from the class during the preliminary observation sessions showed a mean output of approximately 5 written words per minute. During one of the first game sessions this had improved to a mean of approximately 13 written words. However, the number of spelling errors, despite the big increase in output, had hardly changed.

Some of the children were asked their opinion of the game and the vast majority were approving. All of those approving commented upon the fact that the quietness that prevailed enabled them to concentrate and get on with their work without interruption. One issue which was surprising was the effectiveness of housepoints. It had been supposed that some stronger back-up reward would be needed to make the game effective. Perhaps the housepoints worked so well because the intervention took place shortly after the system had been introduced into the school and because it, in turn, was backed up by the award of badges.

RPI games can be implemented equally well in maths lessons as in English lessons as this next study shows. A class of 21 first- and second-year juniors were observed, using OPTIC, during maths lessons. Following five preliminary observations, RPI was initiated based on four rules which were not, on this occasion, negotiated but were decided by the class teacher, a female probationer. (As we have said, in our view negotiation of class rules is a preferable strategy.) The rules were displayed on the classroom wall. In addition a version of the timer game was implemented. Once again, a cassette tape was played which gave out a bleep at random intervals averaging once per minute. The teacher observed one of the three class groups, in random order, each time the bleep sounded. If all children on that table were keeping the rules they were awarded a point which was shown by moving a bead on an abacus in full view of the class.

Each group was observed ten times in each half-hour lesson and if they scored seven or more points they were rewarded with twenty minutes of free choice activity at the end of the day. Praise for rule-keeping and ignoring of infractions was practised as is usual in RPI. Following five lessons of the RPI game, the teacher went back to her normal teaching style and two more observations were made. On-task behaviour averaged 60% during preliminary observations but rose to 82% during the RPI game, falling back to 67% when the game was discontinued. Teacher praise increased and use of reprimands fell during the RPI game phase.

This type of RPI game strategy has been replicated many times and we give a few more examples, with variations, below. An early replication study was with a class of 7-9 year-olds and their teacher. The mixed class included fifteen 7-8 year-olds and eight 8-9 year-olds. The class teacher, a female graduate with five years experience, had no major problems regarding class control but had found the class difficult at the start of the year. Consequently, she decided to employ an RPI game with her class.

Average on-task behaviour at first was around 57% but rose to just over 91% following the introduction of the RPI game. Negative teacher responses to both social and academic behaviour dropped markedly whilst a clear increase in positive responses to social behaviour was in evidence.

The children's enjoyment of this device was obvious and on several occasions they were observed to be "policing" the game by putting their fingers to their lips to quieten individuals who might be breaking the rules. They also spoke in quieter voices when approaching the teacher and waited until they reached her desk before they spoke to her. A major disappointment, however, linked to the teacher's manifest inability to generalise her praise, was that the children quickly returned to their normal noisy out of seat behaviour once the game was over. In other words the teacher failed to generalise the new behaviour to situations other than the game.

The same procedures were tried out with two groups in another primary school, this time with a group of 27 first- and second-year children and with a second group of 25 third- and fourth-year pupils. The game was played when they were taught by the same teacher, an experienced woman graduate, in maths (for the younger group) and in language studies (for the older group). The same three rules were in operation for both and these were: we get on quietly with our work, we try not to interrupt and we wait quietly when we are waiting (in a queue) to have our work marked. The rules were displayed prominently.

Once the game was in operation the pupils' on-task behaviour rose from 77% to 96% in the younger class and from 57% to 94% with the older ones. The teacher's behaviour also changed. With the younger group she managed to reduce her negatives for conduct from an average of about 10 to zero and for academic work from 8 to 3. Her positives applied to conduct increased from 1, on average, to 13 and her positives to academic work increased from about 4 to 10. A similar, but not quite so marked an effect was found in her responses to the other class also.

The same device has also been found to be effective with younger children as two quite independent studies carried out with children aged 5 to 6 clearly demonstrate. In both cases rules were discussed and formulated under the guidance of teachers who felt that they were spending too much time attending to minor disciplinary matters. In one of the classes the teacher used Unifix blocks to indicate when the children had scored a point for playing the game and keeping the rules. She arranged for children who reached a certain score to choose favourite games to play from a special shelf in the classroom for the last ten minutes of the morning programme. In this class on-task behaviour rose from 58% to 71% when the game was being played. The teacher's ratio of positives to negatives also rose so that she now gave two and a half times as many positives as negatives whilst the game was in progress.

In the other class it was possible to trace not only what happened when the game was being played but what happened when it was removed again. The on-task behaviour in this class rose from 46% to 74% when the game was being played and then fell again to 61% when the teacher ceased to operate it. In parallel with these changes in pupil behaviour the teacher's ratio of positives to negatives also changed.

The same game strategy has been employed in a school for children with learning difficulties. The group this time was of 15 children between the ages of 9 and 12. Before the game was played their on-task behaviour level was 64% but this improved to 82% during the intervention. Once again, the idea of the game appealed strongly to the children who often asked if they could play the game after a lesson had begun and on occasions when the teacher had forgotten about it.

By citing so many examples of RPI, including games, in action we have tried to demonstrate the robustness of this strategy and to show how it may be applied successfully in many different teaching contexts with pupils of all ages. In our view RPI is to be recommended to all teachers as a general procedure for improving clasroom behaviour.

Before leaving the topic of games, another and slightly different type of game is worth mentioning: "beat the buzzer". This game was played in a nursery with 20 three and four year-olds. There were two adults with this group and the children were observed through a one-way screen. The teachers were concerned at the great amount of time spent clearing up the room after certain activities.

The children were told that they would hear a buzzer after a certain time and were challenged to see if they could clear up before it sounded and thus "beat the buzzer". Before the game was instituted the average time taken for clearing up was 17.7 minutes but this reduced to 11.5 minutes once the game began. When the game was no longer in operation, the time for clearing up increased once again, this time to an average of 18.4 minutes.

Involving pupils by using self-recording

Pupils themselves can be directly involved in bringing about behaviour change. Older primary pupils can be encouraged to monitor their own behaviour and to determine whether they are on- or off-task, for example, as the following studies illustrate.

The first of these, carried out with one of our students, involved a third-year junior class of thirty pupils, twenty boys and ten girls, aged between 9 and 10 years. Their female teacher had 23 years of teaching experience. Preliminary observations were made of the class using the OPTIC observation schedule. After data had been collected for six sessions over a period of two weeks the teacher showed her class a graph of the preliminary data to see "how hard were they working". This graphical representation of their (low) on-task behaviour, surprised them. They agreed that they would like to do something about it and so the self-recording procedure was introduced.

Every child was provided with a simple recording sheet for each session. For thirty minutes, during the lesson, a tape was played which emitted an audible signal at irregular intervals, but on average once per minute. The children were instructed to record their behaviour, as either on- or off-task, on the self-recording sheet every time that the signal was heard.

To enable children to decide whether or not they were on-task, the teacher negotiated a set of positive rules with them. These rules were: we remain in our seats when we do boardwork, we put up our hands when we want help and we can only come out to get equipment during the investigation task. The rules were not displayed on the blackboard, but the teacher reminded children of them before each lesson. Children who had been on-task 30 times won three housepoints. Those with 29 ticks won two housepoints whilst those who were on-task 25 to 28 times won one housepoint. No child ever failed to score above 25.

In the final phase of the study three further observation sessions were completed during one week without self-recording. The teacher alone carried out the observations and at the end she showed the children the graph of their on-task behaviour (which had increased) and praised them. She then invited them to try to maintain their high on-task rate without listening to the signal and recording themselves.

On-task behaviour during the preliminary observations averaged only 64% but increased markedly to 96% when self-recording was introduced. When self-recording was discontinued the average on-task level fell back to 85%. These results indicate a clear, immediate and enduring effect for self-recording. An interesting side-effect of this study was that negative teacher responses also declined appreciably during self-recording since there was so little inappropriate behaviour to criticise.

During the final phase the level of on-task behaviour fell, providing evidence for the effectiveness of the strategy, but remained relatively high, providing some evidence for maintenance and generalisation. This may have been partly due to the set of rules used as a frame of reference for the children, which had allowed them to decide whether, or not, they were on-task and which were still in force.

Consequently, we carried out a second study to attempt to replicate these findings without employing rules, using three mixed-ability second-, third- and fourth-year junior classes in the same school. These classes were observed during English lessons only. In addition to the class as a whole, three target individuals from each class were observed individually. These target children were selected by their teachers because they were perceived as wasting a lot of time in off-task behaviours. The third-year class consisted of 21 children, 12 boys and 9 girls between 9 and 10 years of age, and their female teacher. The fourth-year class comprised 26 children, 12 girls and 14 boys aged 10 to 11 years and the second year class consisted of 28 pupils, 16 boys and 12 girls, aged between 8 and 9 years. Both these classes were taught by men. Once again, all three classes were observed using the OPTIC schedule. Preliminary observations were carried out for differing numbers of sessions for each class before the self-recording strategy was introduced.

Again the teachers showed the children a graphical representation of their own on-task behaviour and discussed with them the importance of being on-task. In introducing the self-recording treatment, the teachers were asked to a) define clearly what they meant by on- and off-task behaviour b) tell children how to mark their self-recording sheets c) model for them what they were supposed to do using the tape-recorder with the audible signal and the self-recording sheet and d) ask children to repeat the definitions and instructions.

The relatively low averages for on-task behaviour during preliminary observations for all classes confirmed the need for some sort of strategy to be implemented. Self-recording contributed to an increase in average on-task behaviour for all classes: from 72% to 83% in the third-year class; from 64% to 93% in the fourth-year class and from 65% to 87% in the second-year class. Further, follow-up observations of the second-year class when self-recording was discontinued showed a subsequent decrease in on-task behaviour to 69%. Of the nine individual target children observed, eight showed evidence for clear gains in average on-task behaviour as a result of self-recording. The amount of work produced by the three target children in the second-year class was also examined. The average number of words written in half an hour during preliminary observations was 81. This rose rising to 127 during self-recording and fell to 99 during follow-up observations.

Positive Teaching contracts

These examples of self-recording show how pupils experiencing behaviour difficulties can be directly involved in Positive Teaching interventions to improve their own behaviour. Another useful Positive Teaching technique which also involves pupils themselves, and which has some similarity to RPI and games, is behavioural contracting. Some teachers have used what they choose to call contracting for years by compelling children to adhere to certain rules which they impose and by attaching penalties to follow if they are broken. But this is not what we mean by contracting. A Positive Teaching contract is a negotiated agreement entered into freely by all parties and which has clear benefits for all. Ideally, a contract is to be negotiated between a child or a group aware of a learning or behaviour problem and a teacher who is prepared to help. Most children who have such a problem, despite all appearances to the contrary, usually recognise it and are prepared to co-operate if an adult shows sympathy and a willingness to help.

Once it has been agreed that a problem exists the teacher, for it is the adult who will have to take the initiative, should discuss it with the child or the group and agree upon its nature. Then an agreed target for improvement must be negotiated and a statement drawn up. For example, it may be agreed that Adrian will not get out of his seat without permission more than five times in a lesson during the next week. Then some reward acceptable to the pupil must be agreed which will follow if he meets his target. All this must be set down properly, in typewritten form if at all possible, and signed by both parties and as many witnesses as possible. The target should be set so that it is almost certain to be achieved. At the end of the agreed period and this should be short (no longer than two weeks) the reward must follow and another, similar contract be set up. If the early targets are reached fairly easily, and this is what we are aiming for, they can be made gradually more taxing but they must never be too difficult as it is essential for the subject to keep on winning. By degrees the problem will be seen to diminish and the contracts may then cease. Of course, when the contract is kept successfully and the reward is given it must be backed up with recognition of effort, praise for achievement and so on because we want the improved behaviour of work effort to be maintained in the future by all such naturally occurring forms of positive reinforcement.

The various studies reported in this chapter provide convincing evidence of the effectiveness of Positive Teaching methods with primary pupils of all ages. What we are advocating here is that teachers can be both firm and positive. Neither harsh, authoritarian repression nor cloying, patronising sentimentality are congruent with the goals of real education. Our research has shown that teachers can learn to be more effective managers of pupil behaviour by following the principles and procedures of Positive Teaching. In the final section of this chapter we will describe the training package we have developed for primary teachers through which such skills can be learned.

Training teachers to be more positive

There can no longer be any real doubt about the effectiveness of Positive Teaching approaches to problems of classroom order and discipline in primary schools. Primary school teachers can become much more effective managers of classroom behaviour when instructed in the use of Positive Teaching techniques. During the course of our research it rapidly became clear to us that an in-service course by which groups of teachers could be trained effectively was very much needed. To this end, we set up the Positive Teaching Project at the Centre for Child Study in 1981, funded initially by the Schools Council.

We would like to conclude this introduction to Positive Teaching with a description of the training package we have developed for primary teachers. It is based on two important assumptions. First, in order to change their pupils' classroom behaviour teachers must change their own ways of responding to pupils by learning new skills of classroom management. The second assumption follows closely from this: it is only by observing and recording changes in teacher and pupil behaviour that we can claim success for the effectiveness of our training courses. Consequently, the development of our training package has been directly governed by the results of successive evaluations based upon classroom observations. In large part the content of our package draws upon the programmes of experimental and observational classroom research we have already described.

The course we have developed is an in-service training package for primary and middle school teachers entitled the Behavioural Approach to Teaching Package or BATPACK. (We subsequently went on to develop a parallel package for secondary school teachers entitled BATSAC: the Behavioural Approach to Teaching Secondary Aged Children.) BATPACK is a skills-based course to be run on site for the whole staff in a primary school. It is made clear to teachers that BATPACK aims to teach only basic positive skills for managing classroom behaviours (it does not attempt to turn teachers into therapists) and teachers are required to contract that they will attend all sessions and complete all assignments.

The course is designed to be taught by a tutor who has attended one of our tutor training courses. Tutors must have a good working knowledge of Positive Teaching and its applications in schools. Many are educational psychologists but we are also beginning to train more teachers who have followed advanced courses in Positive Teaching. At the training course, which lasts about six hours, tutors receive a copy of a manual which contains all the detailed instructions necessary for a trained tutor to run a course.

The BATPACK course consists of six one-hour sessions called units taught at weekly intervals. A session length of one hour was judged to be as much as most teachers could tolerate at the end of a hard teaching day. The six sessions also fit neatly into a half-term. We decided to operate within these practical constraints and limited our course accordingly. Each unit has its own set of notes which teachers complete during the session. BATPACK units have been planned so that teachers do not just sit and listen to an expert giving advice. In every session course members will find themselves involved in observing, judging and commenting on important behaviour management issues. Many of these are based on video-taped sequences of classroom interactions. During the weekdays, between sessions, they will be observing carefully what is going on in their own classrooms and trying out the various strategies suggested in the previous units. In the weekly BATPACK sessions time is always given for exchange of experiences in applying the suggested strategies and for more general discussion. Encouragement is also given for questions, criticisms and comment so that there are many opportunities for teachers to learn from each other. BATPACK is, after all, the outcome of lengthy development in which feedback from teachers has played an important part. Above all, we would like to stress that standing back from your daily work and considering some of your problems afresh in collaboration with your colleagues is not only fruitful but fun.

Each unit has accompanying course reading and a research note in which an attempt is made to supply some of the theoretical material which will inform the practical skills learned in the unit and which provide the reading assignment for the week. In the last unit an attempt is made to review all the skills and techniques which have been covered and to present some successful classroom strategies tried out by other teachers in primary schools.

BATPACK concentrates upon improving the teacher's ability to manage the classroom situation as a whole rather than the behavioural/learning problems of particular children. It attempts to do this by helping teachers to define clearly the commonest classroom behaviour problems and to observe them carefully, whilst concentrating upon positive measures to bring about change. BATPACK attempts to change teachers' responses to their classes principally by skilful attention to the teaching context and by being more positive towards specifically defined pupil behaviours which they wish to encourage. In addition to specific skills, techniques and procedures, BATPACK also teaches the general principles of Positive Teaching. This enables teachers to use positive methods creatively as well as being able to follow our proven procedures in appropriate situations. More specifically, the contingent and effective use of praise is emphasised. Teachers are also taught related skills such as effective rule setting, whilst video-tapes of classes are used to train teachers in how to "catch them being good" (i.e. to find appropriate times for praise). Various techniques are practised by which teacher praise can be increased and made more effective.

BATPACK has been subject to continual and continuing change and modification during its development. We will not detail the changes here but BATPACK progressed through several revisions before we were sufficiently satisfied to release it for more general use. All teachers who have taken part in BATPACK courses so far have helped in its evaluation and, hence, its development. Since our aim has been to train teachers to be more positive the main focus of our attempts at evaluation has been to see, quite simply, whether BATPACK does, in fact, bring about change in teacher behaviour.

A number of evaluation studies has now been completed testifying to the effectiveness of BATPACK. The following experimental study involved the comparison of a group of teachers who had experienced a full BATPACK course with a control group in another school who had not. All teachers were observed on three separate occasions using OPTIC, both before and after a seven to eight week interval, during which the experimental group received BATPACK training. The control group received one seminar on Positive Teaching during this period and two papers to read which set out the guidelines for the application of these methods in the classroom.

Prior to BATPACK training the two groups of teachers were very similar in terms of their use of approval and disapproval. Rates of disapproval to both academic and social behaviour were very low in both groups, as was approval of social behaviour. Approval for academic behaviour, however, was (relatively) very high. Average on-task behaviour of the classes was around 75% in both groups, again quite high.

At the end of the experiment the control group had barely changed, except to increase their rates of negative responding to both academic and social behaviour and this was accompanied by a 6% drop in the average on-task behaviour of their classes. Positive responding to both academic and social behaviour was almost identical to the rates found during initial observations. The BATPACK group, however, who had now completed the course, showed marked increases in approval rates and maintained their low levels of negative responding. Positive responses to academic behaviour more than doubled whilst those to social behaviour increased by a factor of one hundred! Whereas, only 10% of the positive responses given before the BATPACK course were accompanied by an explanation, over 35% of positive responses after the course were rule-related, accompanied by a reason or used as an example to encourage others. (We refer to these sorts of more effective positive responses as REX responses, as discussed in Chapter Four.) On-task behaviour in the classes in the BATPACK group increased, on average, by 9% to 84% (compared with a decline to 68% in the control classes). In short, after the BATPACK course was completed there were significant differences on all of the measures favouring the BATPACK group, showing them to be more positive, less negative and with higher on-task behaviour levels among their pupils.

Turning now to the results for individuals it was shown that all teachers in the BATPACK group doubled (or in two cases almost doubled) their previous rates for use of positives. In the control group only a few minor increases in positive behaviour were apparent. On-task behaviour was seen to increase in five out of six experimental classes, with the sixth class maintaining its already high on-task level (81%). In the control group on-task behaviour fell in all classes except one.

All the teachers who took the course completed (anonymously) the BATPACK questionnaire. All of them regarded BATPACK more favourably at the end than at the beginning and all were prepared to recommend the course to colleagues. All believed that their own responses to children had improved and that they had increased their rates of positive responding. They were less sure about the levels of their negative responses. Some of the teachers reported that they had attempted to change antecedents; for example, four of them had set up rules in their classrooms. Comments about the structure of the course were very favourable and attendance at the course was excellent; one teacher only was absent for one session. (Typically attendance rates for BATPACK have been in the high 90s%, infrequent absences invariably resulting from sickness or family crisis.)

Two subsequent, independent evaluations of BATPACK were undertaken without any direct involvement by either of its authors. The first of these was carried out in Scotland and observations were made before and after a BATPACK course taught to all twelve teachers in a school. Reports from the teachers after the course were almost entirely favourable whilst the tutors reported, "We feel that it (BATPACK) has long-term positive effects for all concerned". Eight of the teachers were prepared to be observed and this observation was carried out for each teacher three times both before and after the course. The results showed that for academic behaviour positive responses hardly changed but there was a significant decrease in negative responding. For social behaviour, the results were highly significant, positive responses rising by more than four times and negative responses falling to less than half of the pre-course levels. Moreover, average pupil time on task rose dramatically by 16%, from 68% to 84%.

In the second of these evaluations, nine class teachers took part in the course and six of them were observed by the independent observer. Teachers' positive responses to children's academic behaviour increased substantially and significantly whilst the positive responses to social behaviour also increased, though not so greatly. The use of more effective positive (REX) responses, especially those addressed to academic behaviour, increased dramatically by a factor of eight. Similarly, teachers' negative responding dropped sharply, especially in relation to children's social behaviour. Average on-task behaviour for the six classes again increased appreciably by 16%, from 67% to 73%.

Another small-scale study was carried out in a small primary school in Birmingham where the whole staff attended a BATPACK course. Five of the teachers attending agreed to be observed. Observations of teacher and class behaviours were collected before and following the course using our OPTIC schedule. Before the course, the teachers' overall use of negative statements (repri-mands) was greater than their use of positive statements (praise). Following the course over three times as many praise statements as reprimands were employed, on average. All teachers increased their use of praise, except one whose level was already far higher than that of the other teachers. All teachers dramatically de-creased their use of reprimands especially those directed at social behaviour. Pupil on-task behaviour following BATPACK increased, on average, from 67% to 84%. Gains ranged from 4% to 28% and averaged 17%. In other words, children on average spent 25% more time working, following BATPACK training.

An attempt was also made to collect evidence for change in quantity and quality of work produced by the pupils. To this end, teachers were asked to set given essay topics to their classes with a thirty-minute time limit. Only the teacher of the top junior class (of 10-11 year olds), however, was successful in collecting a sample of essays before and after the course. The mean on-task behaviour for this class for the writing session before the course was 71% compared with 99% for the session following completion of the course. In the pre-course session, the children produced a mean of 116 words in the half-hour session, whilst in the session following the course this had risen by over 30% to a mean of 152 words. Clearly, increases in academic behaviour coincided with increases in on-task behaviour.

These findings of increased productivity have been confirmed in a larger-scale study involving the whole staff of a large primary school who received BATPACK training in two groups. Of the 23 teachers attending the courses, 22 completed our pre- and post-training questionnaires. Nine agreed to be observed before and after BATPACK training and twelve teachers agreed to collect samples of their pupils' written work before and after they (the teachers) had taken the course.

The 22 teachers demonstrated a clear positive shift in attitude towards Positive Teaching methods after taking the course and all of them said that they would recommend BATPACK training to a colleague. Almost all thought that they had increased their use of positive responses and most thought that they had decreased their use of negatives. Similarly, the group as a whole were far more likely to select answers based on Positive Teaching approaches to solving classroom behaviour problems after the course than before.

Once again, classroom observations showed that the nine teachers observed had increased their overall rates of positive responding, on average by 60% and had reduced their negative responding to only 30% of pre-course levels. Except for one class, where the pupil on-task level was already in excess of 90%, all classes increased their levels of on-task behaviour by an average of over 13%, from just over 68% to nearly 82%. Finally, the amount of written work produced by pupils increased significantly after teachers had completed the course. Prior to the courses, pupils averaged 58 written words per 15 minutes but afterwards this rose to 73, an increase of over 25%. Thus, we have increasing evidence that BATPACK training successfully changes teacher behaviour which, in turn, influences children's behaviour. Following our courses the amount of time pupils spend on-task increases substantially and this is accompanied by increased work output.

There are now about a thousand trained and registered tutors qualified to teach BATPACK, not only in the UK but also in Australia, New Zealand, Hong Kong and Canada. Reports of its effectiveness in practice have continued but we have been developing the package further. We are currently carrying out trials with an extensively revised five-unit version of our primary package. The results of a recent study in which seven teachers were observed before and after training with this new version have been most encouraging. Not only were the teachers very enthusiastic but their behaviour had changed markedly. Their use of positives increased substantially, so that they were subsequently using twenty times as many positives to social behaviour as before and many times more REX responses. Negatives fell to half their original levels. Every class improved on their previous level of on-task behaviour as a result of the course, increases ranging from 6% to 20% and averaging 13%.

BATPACK was designed specifically to help teachers with general problems of classroom management in mainstream primary schools. However, one of the major concerns of many teachers is the presence of one or two really troublesome pupils. Such children can be very disruptive and cause a great deal of trouble to an already harassed teacher. This is the reason that BATPACK concentrates upon dealing with the class as a whole for we would argue that with good general classroom management the problems raised by pupils who are especially troublesome are much more manageable. Nevertheless, the problem pupils, like the poor, will always be with us and so we are beginning to develop a further package to help primary teachers deal with them, currently codenamed BRATPACK!

The Elton Report and subsequent policy decisions made by the Secretary of State for Education and Science have stressed the importance of effective classroom behaviour management in relation to the professional competence of teachers. Strong recommendations have been made about the provision of training for teachers in this area both at pre-service and in-service levels. In this book we have tried to convince readers of the benefits of Positive Teaching in relation to effective classroom behaviour management. We have discussed the basic operating principles, we have described our surveys and observational studies and we have reported numerous demonstration studies of Positive Teaching in practice in the classroom. We hope that reading this book will whet your appetite for Positive Teaching but reading is no substitute for doing. So why not put Positive Teaching to the test? Try it out for yourself in class!

Further reading

The original RPI game study with primary pupils is reported in :

Merrett, F. and Wheldall, K. (1978). Playing the game: a behavioural approach to classroom management. *Educational Review, 30,* 41-50.

The study on pupil self-recording is described fully in:

Wheldall, K. and Panagopoulou-Stamatelatou, A. (1989). The effects of pupil self-recording of on-task behaviour in primary classes. Centre for Child Study, University of Birmingham.

Numerous case studies of interventions carried out by teachers in their own classrooms using Positive Teaching methods are described in:

Merrett, F. E. (1986). *Encouragement Works Better Than Punishment* (second edition). Birmingham: Positive Products.

Wheldall, K. and Merrett, F. (1984). *Positive Teaching: the behavioural approach.* London: Allen & Unwin, reprinted 1989 by Positive Products, Birmingham.

The development of the Positive Teaching training packages is described in:

Wheldall, K. and Merrett, F. (1987). Training teachers to use the behavioural approach to classroom management: the development of BATPACK. In Wheldall, K. (ed.) *The Behaviourist in the Classroom.* London: Allen & Unwin.

Wheldall, K. and Merrett, F. (1988). Packages for training teachers in classroom behaviour management: BATPACK, BATSAC and the Positive Teaching Packages. *Support for Learning, 3,* 86-92.

INDEX

ABC of Positive Teaching 18-22
academic
 behaviour 11, 14, 15, 28
 engagement 50
 knowledge 18
 learning and social behaviour
  11, 15, 18, 28, 42, 79, 85-6,
  101-2
 skills 11, 14, 18
 work 23-4, 25, 75, 79-80, 87, 93
accentuating the positive 65-6
aggression 5, 7, 9
answering questions 12, 27
antecedents 12-13, 18, 35-6, 49-
 50, 52, 79, 82-3, 99 see also
 contexts; settings
appropriate behaviour 12, 14, 17-
 34, 53-4, 69, 76
 increasing 21, 53
 maintaining 75
 recognising 27-8
 responding to 29-34
approval 19, 20, 23-4, 57, 99
 by peers 84
attention seeking behaviour 20,
 26, 63, 84
attitudes, authoritarian 2-3, 95
avoidance
 behaviour 20-1, 26
 of conflict 22, 26, 54, 61, 63

back-up reinforcers 87, 90, 94
behaviour 18-19
 academic 11, 14, 15, 28
 appropriate see appropriate
  behaviour
 attention seeking 20, 26, 59
 avoidance 20-1, 26

change 12, 13, 22, 65 see also
 case studies; maintaining
 behaviour change
 classroom 12, 23-4, 35, 76, 83
 disruptive 17, 22, 33, 43, 51, 64
 hyperactive 11, 32
 improvement in 28, 31
 inappropriate 13, 14, 24, 35, 81
 learning of 12, 22, 76
 maintenance of 13, 21, 26, 75,
  77-8, 92
 non work-related 17, 19
 on-task see on-task behaviour
 out of seat (OOS) 5, 15, 42,
 social 11, 15, 23, 26, 28, 34, 79
  see also social behaviour and
  learning
 troublesome see troublesome
  behaviour
Behavioural Approach to
 Teaching Package, The
 (BATPACK) 96-103
 evaluation of 98-102
 questionnaire 99
 training courses 95-8, 104
Behavioural Approach to
 Teaching Secondary Aged
 Children, The (BATSAC)
 58, 99
behavioural
 contracting 94-5, 96
 objectives 22
blame 67
bribery 15-16

case studies in
 infants classes 48-9, 66-7, 71,
  79-80

lower junior classes 46-7, 49-50, 80-1, 85-6, 87-9, 89-90
nursery classes 85, 90-1
other classes 90
upper junior classes 39, 41-3, 49-50, 51-2, 62-3, 71-3, 81-3, 86-7, 91-3
catching children being good 84, 97
categories of misbehaviour 5
Centre for Child Study, University of Birmingham 95
charts 74, 79-80
classrooms
  arrangement of 39-44
  behaviour 12, 23-4, 35, 76, 83
  behaviour and academic learning 11, 15, 18, 28, 42, 79, 85-6, 101-2
  contexts 12-13, 18, 35-55
  control 4-5, 10-11, 44, 54, 58
  movement in 40
  rules *see* rules
  seating *see* seating arrangements
  strategies 70, 76-95
competition 74-5, 83
conflict, avoidance of 22, 26, 54, 61, 63
consequences 12, 13, 18, 19-22, 65, 79
  aversive 13, 21, 57
  natural 53, 62, 78
  negative 25, 69
  neutral 20
  punishing 12, 20, 25, 57
  rewarding 12, 20, 25, 68 *see also* reinforcement
consistency 73, 77, 78

contexts 12-13, 18, 35-55 *see also* antecedents; settings
contingent reinforcement 31, 51, 65, 73, 83
contracts 94-5, 96
control
  in classrooms 4-5, 10-11, 44, 58
  group 98, 99
cues 36, 69, 87
curriculum issues 37-9

definitions
  of behaviour 11, 18-19, 29-30, 81
  objective 4, 19, 97
desist commands 8, 17
disapproval 20, 23-4, 91
Discipline in Schools (The Elton Report) 3, 7, 16, 45, 103
disobedience 5

ecological variables 39-44
educational psychologists 3, 9, 96
Effective Classroom Learning (Wheldall and Glynn) 22, 34
Elton Report, The *(Discipline in Schools)* 3, 7, 16, 45, 103
encouragement 57, 59
English 87, 92, 101
equipment, control of 40, 45-6
evaluation of BATPACK 98-102
evaluative statements 78
explanatory fictions 9, 11, 15, 19, 32
extrinsic rewards 29, 32
extroversion 9

fading of reinforcement 21-2, 78
feedback 10, 20, 97 *see also*
    reinforcement
flexibility 42, 44
flow diagrams 45, 50
free time 30, 58, 59, 74

games 80-1, 82-3, 86-91, 103
generalisation 83, 89, 92
Grandma's law 30, 51
graphs 91, 93
hand raising 27, 48, 49, 54-5
Her Majesty's Inspectorate 37
hindering other children (HOC)
    5, 6, 7-9, 14, 17, 41, 80
humour 64
hyperactivity 11, 32

idleness 5, 6, 17
ignoring 20, 25, 31, 61, 63-4, 81,
    84
improvement
    in behaviour 28, 31
    in performance 27, 28, 30, 68,
        74-5, 79, 81
independent learners 22, 49-50
infant classes 48-9, 66-7, 71, 79-
    80
Inner London Education Au-
    thority 28
instructions 44-5
intrinsic rewards 32

junior classes *see* case studies
justice 72
justifying our actions 13-15

labelling 9, 11, 13, 31, 32, 68
language learning 85, 89

learners, independent 22, 49-50
learning 11, 15, 18, 30, 85, 89

lessons
    flow of 44-52
    preparation for 37-8
letter home 55-6, 59-60, 74
Locke, John (quoted) 57

maintaining behaviour change
    13, 21, 26, 75, 77-8, 92
matching 14-15, 37, 41, 50, 56, 60
mathematics 87-8, 89
misbehaviour 5, 28, 84
modelling 58, 93
motivation 17, 51, 55, 59, 73-4,
    76

National Union of Teachers
    (NUT) 1
negative reinforcement 20-1
negativeness of teachers 6, 17, 26
negotiation of rules 53-5, 83, 91,
    94
noise levels 5, 52, 82
number learning 85
nursery classes 85, 90-1

*OPTIC :Observing Pupils and
    Teachers In Classrooms*
    (Merrett and Wheldall) 23,
    98, 100-1
    used in infant classes 66, 71
    used in junior classes 49, 62,
        73, 87, 91, 93
    used in nurseries 85
objectives, behavioural 22
observation 33
    of classes 86, 90, 95-6

of colleagues 33, 65, 95
importance of 10, 11, 18-19, 29-30, 47, 48
schedules 33
of self 33, 65
Observing Pupils and Teachers In Classrooms (OPTIC) (Merrett and Wheldall) *see* OPTIC
On Education (Locke, J.) 57
on report 60
on-task behaviour 14, 23, 27, 70-1
in infant classes 66-7
in lower junior classes 80, 81, 85-6, 88-9
in upper junior classes 41-2, 52, 62-3, 71-2, 73, 86-7, 91-3
opinions
of pupils 60
of teachers 23, 60
order in classrooms 4-5
out of seat behaviour (OOS) 5, 15, 42

parents, co-operation with 10
pay-off 32
peer approval 84
pencil rally 46
performance, improvement in *see* improvement in performance
physical
aggression 5, 7, 9
education 46-7, 58
violence 1, 7, 8
pin-pointing 19, 27, 30, 76-7
Plowden Report 41

points 58, 59, 74, 86-7, 88, 90, 92
see also tokens
positive
feedback 10, 20
reinforcement *see* reinforcement, positive
Positive Teaching: the behavioural approach (Wheldall and Merrett) 33, 34
Positive Teaching
ABC of 18-22
principles of 11-13, 97
Positive Teaching Project 95
positives *see also* ratios of positives and negatives
accentuating 65-6
improving 65-73
Praise and Rewards Attitude Questionnaire (PRAQ) 59
praise 15, 19, 22-4, 59, 81, 86
contingent 73
effectiveness of 65-73, 97-8
enhancing rates of 50, 57-8, 65-73, 98
private 58, 62, 66
supplementing 73-5
prevalence of misbehaviour 3-8
principles of Positive Teaching 11-13, 97
Professional Association of Teachers (PAT) 1
projects 51
prompting 31, 61, 75, 83
psychologists, educational 3, 9, 96
punctuality 5
punishment 20, 25-6, 36
corporal 18, 26
effective 59-60

pupil opinions on 60
side effects of 20-1, 25-6

questionnaires 1, 4, 99, 101
questions, answering of 12, 27
queuing 48, 49

REX responses 67-8, 71, 99, 100, 102
raising hands 27, 48, 49, 54-5
randomisation 86-7
ratios of positives and negatives 24, 62-4, 69-70, 88-90, 99-100, 101-2
reading 11, 38-9, 46, 47, 51, 55, 59, 81
recording 47, 73, 74-5, 95
  behaviour 69, 77, 86
  progress 75
  self *see* self-recording
  signal for 79, 86, 91, 93
reinforcement 31, 35, 69, 76-8
  back-up 87, 90, 94
  consistent 73, 77, 78
  contingent 31, 51, 65, 73, 83
  continuous 21, 78
  effective 59, 62, 97-8
  fading of 21-2, 78
  frequency of 21
  immediate 76-7
  intermittent 21, 78
  natural 57, 62, 78, 83, 95
  negative 20-1
  positive 20, 21, 29-31, 32-3, 57-8, 62, 81
  primary 58, 59
  schedules 21-2
  social 20, 29, 30, 31-2, 57, 65-6, 82-3

relationships between teachers and pupils 1-2, 25
remedial pupils 32, 83
reprimands 8, 17, 22-6, 33, 50
  effectiveness of 61-5
  side effects of 20, 25-6
response
  cost 21
  rates 24, 70, 92, 101-2
responses
  REX 67-8, 71, 99, 100, 102
  of teachers 17, 23-4, 35, 70, 92
  variety in 65
responsive teaching 11
return rate of survey schedules 4-5
rewards 15, 20, 30, 47, 66, 74, 94
  effective 25, 59-60
  extrinsic 29, 32
  intrinsic 32
  pupil opinions on 60
routines, importance of 40, 46, 48
rules
  classroom 9, 10, 52-5, 67-8, 81, 99
  criteria for 53
  ground 78
  negotiation of 53-5, 83, 91, 94
  school 24
rules, praise and ignoring 64, 83-91

sanctions 17, 24, 26, 60, 61
schedules 5, 33
school
  policy 82
  rules *see* rules

Schools Council 95
seating arrangements 9, 10, 13,
    36, 40-4, 46, 86
secondary
    pupils 59, 78
    schools 60
    teachers 6
self
    criticism 68
    observation 33, 65,
    recording 74-5, 91-3, 94, 104
settings 13, 40-4 *see also* antece-
    dents; contexts
sex differences
    in pupil behaviour 6, 42-3
    and seating 42-3
    in teacher behaviour 5, 24
shaping 58
signal, time 79, 86, 91, 93
skills learning 13, 22, 30, 97
slowness 5, 6
social behaviour and learning 11,
    15, 18, 28, 42, 79, 85-6, 101-2
stars 28, 58, 74, 79-80 *see also*
    tokens
stress among teachers 2, 3, 6-8,
    17, 25, 26
supplementing praise 73-5
symptom substitution 15

tally-counters 33, 70
tallying 33, 81
talking out of turn (TOOT) 5, 6,
    7-9, 17, 19
tape recording 70, 93
target children 86, 92, 93
targets 68, 94
teachers 1
    attention of 20, 26, 48, 59, 84

authority of 54, 61, 95
behaviour of 22-5, 62-4, 98
consensus among 8, 22, 23
imagination of 33, 79, 97
initiative of 33, 79
negativeness of 6, 17, 25
omniscience of 29
opinions of 23, 30-1, 56
and parents 10-11, 25
positive 74, 95-7, 98
professionalism of 17, 64, 79
reactions of 17, 20, 27, 64
responses to children 17, 23-5,
    33, 70, 92
secondary 6
skills of 11, 27, 33, 62, 97
survey of 23-4
training of 95-102, 103
teaching 9
    new behaviour 12, 22, 26, 70,
        98
    new skills 22, 30
    practice 66
    responsive 11
    styles 63
tidiness 5, 79-80
time
    free (extra) 30, 58, 59, 74
    wasting 79-80, 85, 90-1, 92-3
timer
    game 76, 80-1
    kitchen 79
tokens 28, 58, 74, 80, 81, 86-7 *see
    also* points
topic work 51
touch, use of 66-7
training of teachers 95-102, 103
treats, special 30, 74, 85

troublesome behaviour 1-11, 17,
    18, 94

USSR (Uninterrupted Sustained
    Silent Reading) 38-9

verbal interaction 72
video tapes, use of 96, 97
violence 1, 7, 8
visual records 74

waiting time 49-50
wall charts 74
wasting time 79-80, 85, 90-1, 92-3
work
    academic *see* academic work
    additional 51
    cards 41
    collaborative 41
    improvement in 27, 28, 30, 68,
        74-5, 79, 81
    levels 10, 44
    output 39, 80, 93
    projects 51
    sheets 45
    written 81, 85, 101, 102
writing 11, 81, 101